SUPER
STRUCTURES

LONDON, NEW YORK, MELBOURNE, MUNICH, and DELHI

Author Samone Bos
Consultant Philip Wilkinson

Senior Editor Andrea Mills
Senior Art Editor Sheila Collins
Managing Editor Linda Esposito
Managing Art Editor Diane Thistlethwaite

Publishing Manager Andrew Macintyre
Category Publisher Laura Buller
Design Development Manager
Sophia Tampakopoulos Turner
Production Controller Sarah Hughes
Production Editor Andy Hilliard, Laragh Kedwell
Picture Research Harriet Mills
Jacket Editor Mariza O'Keeffe
Jacket Designer Hazel Martin
US Editor Margaret Parrish

Illustrations Inklink Firenze

First published in the United States in 2008
by DK Publishing
375 Hudson Street, New York, New York 10014

Copyright © 2008 Dorling Kindersley Limited
08 09 10 11 12 10 9 8 7 6 5 4 3 2 1
WD166 – 10/08

A catalog record for this book
is available from the Library of Congress.
ISBN: 978-0-7566-4088-0

Jacket color reproduction and inside color reproduction
by Media Development & Printing Ltd.
Printed and bound in China by Hung Hing

**Discover more at
www.dk.com**

Contents

Pharos of Alexandria
This 400-ft (122-m) lighthouse guided ships from the Mediterranean Sea into the Egyptian city's harbor. The Greek architect Sostratus designed the giant beacon in about 270 BCE. By day, the Sun's rays beamed off a big mirror to create light, while at night, the Pharos was lit by fire.

Mausoleum of Halicarnassus
In about 353 BCE, a monumental marble tomb was built for the Persian King Mausolus in modern-day Turkey. News spread of the 135-ft- (41-m-) high structure by Greek architect Pythius. Soon, the word "mausoleum" was used to describe similar grand funereal crypts.

Great Pyramid of Giza
Completed in about 2560 BCE, Egypt's Great Pyramid is the royal tomb of Pharaoh Khufu. The 455-ft- (138-m-) tall pyramid contains approximately 2.3 million limestone blocks. It is estimated that it took 100,000 laborers more than 20 years to assemble the stunning structure.

Hanging Gardens of Babylon
Babylon's hanging gardens were constructed by King Nebuchadnezzar II in modern-day Iraq in about 600 BCE. These gardens may have been named after the lush vines trailing down the tiered structure, which looked to be suspended in the desert sky.

Colossus of Rhodes
Honoring the Greek sun god Helios, this 100-ft (30-m) bronze statue was built in about 280 BCE. The Colossus stood astride the entrance to Mandraki Harbour in Rhodes, and was the world's tallest statue until an earthquake destroyed it in 226 BCE.

Temple of Artemis
One of the ancient world's largest temples, the Temple of Artemis in Turkey was completed in 550 BCE. Soaring 60 ft (18 m) high, the temple consisted of a colonnade of about 106 columns encircling a marble sanctuary covered by a tiled roof.

Early Greek and Roman scholars wrote travel records describing the world's most magnificent structures, resulting in the famous Seven Wonders of the Ancient World. Today, the only surviving structure is the Great Pyramid of Giza in Egypt, with the others destroyed by time, war, or natural disasters. The only evidence that some of these wonders existed is old literature, so modern archeologists must refer to other buildings of the time to guess at how these structures looked. It has been debated that some wonders may be purely myth and legend.

Statue of Zeus
The people of Olympia in Ancient Greece wanted a temple dedicated to their god Zeus. In about 457 BCE, the sculptor Phidias carved a 40-ft (12-m) ivory statue. Surrounded by classic columns, the throned Zeus had robes made of gold.

Modern wonders

Christ the Redeemer
Standing over Rio de Janeiro in Brazil, Christ the Redeemer is a religious monument on the city's Corcovado Mountain. Officially opened on October 12, 1931, the interior structure was engineered in reinforced concrete, with the outer layers of the 130-ft (39-m) statue carved in soapstone.

Petra
The ancient Nabataean settlement of Petra in Jordan is reached via the Siq, a half-mile (1-km) gorge. The streets are lined with altars, obelisks, temples, and tombs, all carved into sheer rockface. The Treasury, a king's tomb, is 100 ft (30 m) wide and 141 ft (43 m) high.

Taj Mahal
After 12 years of construction, the Taj Mahal complex in Agra, India, was completed in 1648. Its centrepiece is the white marble-tiled mausoleum dedicated to the Mughal emperor Shah Jahan's wife, Mumtaz Mahal. The cube-shaped tomb has four floors, capped by a huge dome.

The Great Wall of China
China's first emperor Qin Shi Huangdi began construction on the Great Wall in about 200 BCE. With fortified walls made of packed-dirt, stonework, and rocks, succeeding dynasties added to the structure over many centuries. Today, it stretches 4,000 miles (6,508 km) east to west.

Machu Picchu
Known as "The Lost City of the Incas," Machu Picchu is a polished-stone complex between two mountains above the Urubamba Valley in Peru. It was built in about 1450 by the Inca Empire, and was brought to public attention in 1911 by US historian Hiram Bingham.

The Colosseum
Completed in 80 CE, the Colosseum was Ancient Rome's premier entertainment venue. Reigning emperors hosted epic contests inside the huge amphitheater, with gladiators (trained fighters) battling in front of up to 50,000 people.

On a planet brimming with spectacular man-made structures, it is not surprising that many are dubbed "The Eighth Wonder of the World" by proud countries and tourist organizations. In modern times, it was often suggested that an official list should be compiled to represent the most stunning and symbolic structures. An international competition known as the New Seven Wonders of the World began in September 1999. One hundred million votes were cast by the general public, with this final list announced in Lisbon, Portugal, on July 7, 2007.

Chichen Itza
Built by the Mayan civilization between 1000 and 1200 CE, El Castillo is part of Mexico's ancient Chichen Itza site. With a temple at the top, the 78-ft (24-m) step-pyramid is dedicated to the feathered-serpent god Kukulcan. Each stone facade has a staircase of 91 steps.

Dracula's Castle

In 1212, Bran Castle was built between Transylvania and Wallachia, now modern-day Romania. Initially a stronghold for the Knights of the Teutonic Order, it was used as a fortress against the invading Ottomans in 1378. The author Bram Stoker based his vampire Count Dracula on the murderous 15th-century Romanian prince Vlad Tepes, who was said to have stayed here, and the building is now known as "Dracula's Castle."

Fortified city

Carcassonne in southern France is a walled city dating back to Roman times. Count's Castle was added to the fortification in the 13th century as the city's administrative center and royal residence. Double walls lined with 53 round towers and battlements were built between 1228 and 1239 to protect the castle, with the added defense of a now-dry moat. Many of the town walls were replaced in the 19th century. Today, the city is a tourist attraction, with hotels and restaurants established inside the walls.

Spis Castle
Looming from a 655-ft (200-m) dolomite rock foundation, Spis Castle in eastern Slovakia was built in the 12th century. Its elevated position and high walls intimidated potential invaders.

Matsumoto Castle
Completed in 1594, Matsumoto Castle in Japan was built on a stone platform surrounded by a moat, to deter attack. The six-floor fortification housed the region's daimyo (feudal ruler) and his guards.

Krak des Chevaliers
A fortress during the Middle Ages, Krak des Chevaliers in Syria was home to the Knights Hospitaller and about 2,000 soldiers. Two defensive walls kept invaders out, with the higher inner wall 100 ft (30 m) thick in some parts.

Jewel in the crown
In 1078, William the Conqueror ordered the construction of a square fortress known as the Tower of London. Over the centuries, the original White Tower was surrounded by more walls and turrets. Home to the Crown Jewels since 1303, the fortress has been a royal home, prison, zoo, treasury, and place of execution.

Castles

Many castles were built in medieval times as protective residences for a reigning monarch, or a stronghold from which a lord could oversee his land. Castle defenses included thick stone walls, gatehouses, moats, and drawbridges, with guards watching from tall towers for approaching invaders. Archers were strategically positioned around these castles, ready to shoot at enemies through small openings in the stonework called "murder holes."

Tourist hit ▶
Each year, 1.3 million tourists visit
this scenic part of Germany and
pass through Neuschwanstein.

On tap ▶
Mineral-rich drinking water was
piped to the castle from a natural
spring 650 ft (200 m) away.

Modern conveniences ▼
Features of the castle included
elevators, automatic flushing
toilets, and a telephone system.

▼ Stage for opera
Ludwig II admired the composer
Richard Wagner, basing the castle's
interior paintings on his operas.

Dinner for one ▶
As Ludwig II dined alone, the
dining room was small compared
to the rest of the castle.

◀ Imitation luxury
Much of the room's grandeur
was an illusion—the pillars and
mosaics were plaster and paint.

Combined influences ▶
From Romanesque to Gothic
and Byzantine, the interior was
a mixture of architectural styles.

Neuschwanstein

Nestled in the Bavarian Alps of Germany, Neuschwanstein was built as the private retreat of King Ludwig II. When work commenced in 1869, the royal ruler requested that the architect Eduard Riedel base his design upon the stage sets of German scenery painter Christian Jank. Outside, the towers and spires were a romantic reinterpretation of a classic medieval castle, yet the interior was equipped with every modern convenience available. In 1886, Ludwig II died with his castle unfinished and cloaked in scaffolding.

Eroding surface ▶
The Alps' harsh wintry climate erodes the soft limestone surface, requiring regular maintenance.

▼ Wagner performance
The castle's first Wagner concert was performed in the Singer's Hall more than 60 years after Ludwig's death.

◀ Limestone exterior
The limestone used to clad the brick exterior was quarried from the nearby town of Alterschrofen.

◀ Gothic grandeur
Over four years, 14 artisans carved the oak that made up the king's Gothic-inspired bedroom.

◀ King's hideaway
With colored lighting and a small waterfall, "The Grotto" was built to resemble a dripstone cave.

◀ Wide windows
When Neuschwanstein was built, the windowpanes were considered very large and extravagant.

Hired help ▲
The reclusive king refused visitors, and had more than 30 servants while he lived in the castle.

◀ Central heating
In freezing winters, the castle was kept warm by a sophisticated central heating system.

▲ Unstable soils
Set on shifting rock, the castle's foundations need constant maintenance to ensure safety.

Laying foundations ▶
The foundation stone was laid in 1869, but the king did not live in the castle until 1884.

Opera enthusiast

When planning Neuschwanstein's construction, King Ludwig II asked the stage scenery designer Christian Jank to create an artwork (above) for the architects to use as their blueprint. Jank was later employed to paint murals of medieval kings, knights, and poets that composer Richard Wagner mentioned in his operas.

WOW!
King Ludwig II used the latest technologies in all areas of his life. He was said to travel by night in high-powered sleighs and coaches, while dressed in historic costume.

Castle grandeur

Featuring a crown protected by fierce animals, the king's personal coat of arms was carved over the castle's main entrance. This led the way into room after room of ornate columns, decorative details, and colorful paintings. A swan crest was also seen regularly throughout the castle. Lohengrin, the hero of Wagner's opera of the same name, was known as the "swan knight" because he sailed in a boat pulled by a swan.

Building blocks

Like the dramatic operas that King Ludwig II admired, the construction of Neuschwanstein Castle was an epic production. Building work commenced on the castle in 1869, with the foundation stone laid on September 5 of that year, and its roofs finally added in 1881. The site has an idyllic outlook over rugged mountain alps and low-lying meadows, yet the remote rocky location was a challenge for the teams of construction staff. Tons of bricks, cement, and Salzburg marble were carted to the site from Bavaria and neighboring lands, with cranes powered by steam engines lifting the materials into place.

Architectural inspiration

Marksburg Castle
Since the 12th century, Marksburg Castle in Germany has dominated the skyline over the Rhine River. During the Middle Ages, the castle expanded from a simple stronghold to an impenetrable medieval fortress.

Krumlov Castle
Dating back to 1240, Krumlov Castle in the Czech Republic stands on a rocky headland over the Vitava River. The grand, Gothic complex contains 40 buildings, five castle courts, and a leafy park. The castle is unusually large compared to the small town it overlooks.

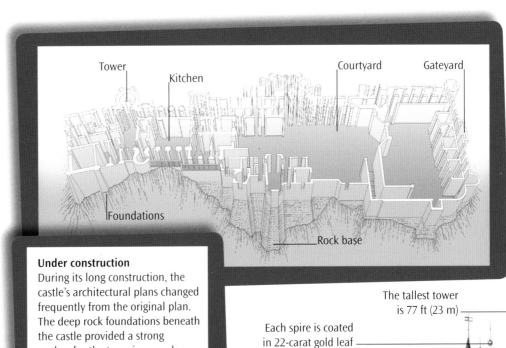

Tower · Kitchen · Courtyard · Gateyard · Foundations · Rock base

Under construction
During its long construction, the castle's architectural plans changed frequently from the original plan. The deep rock foundations beneath the castle provided a strong anchor for the towering wooden scaffolding that surrounded the structure for 15 years.

The tallest tower is 77 ft (23 m)

Each spire is coated in 22-carat gold leaf

Fairytale castle
The Sleeping Beauty Castle at Disneyland theme park in California was based on the design of Neuschwanstein. Opened by Walt Disney on July 17, 1955, the pink and blue fantasy structure includes "fortifications" imitating a traditional Germanic castle, such as watchtowers, turrets, a drawbridge, and moat.

Town hall
Now the town hall, the Palazzo Vecchio in Italy was built for Florence's Signoria (government) in about 1299. The fortresslike structure includes a 308-ft (94-m) tower, with two small prison cells.

History museum
Mexico's National Museum of History was first built as a country house for the Spanish Viceroy (governor) in 1785. The structure has since been a presidential residence, military academy, and astronomical observatory.

Palaces

With different meanings around the world, a palace can be the grand home or administrative chambers of a monarch, head of state, or government official. Traditionally, some imperial palaces included defensive features usually found on a castle, such as a moat and series of gatehouses. These defenses were built to protect the wealthy and powerful occupants, as well as their important documents and priceless heirlooms. Today, many historical palaces have been converted into public buildings and museums, enabling everyone to enjoy the lavish décor and architecture.

Red palace

Meaning "the red" in Arabic, Alhambra in southern Spain is a Moorish palace dating back to 1338. First built to house the Muslim kings of the Nasrid dynasty, the complex contains a mosque and government rooms. Sweeping courtyards, such as the Court of the Lions, feature water basins and fountains surrounded by delicate colonnades.

故宮博物院

Chinese treasure

Once home to 24 emperors from the Qing and Ming dynasties, the Imperial Palace (Forbidden City) in Beijing was the center of the Chinese kingdom from 1420. More than 9,000 rooms are contained within the rectangular compound that stretches ¼ sq miles (0.72 sq km). Today, the palace is a museum housing one million relics of China's ancient culture.

Fit for a king

In 1783, the Grand Palace in Bangkok was built as the official residence of the King of Siam (Thailand). At this time, the outer court contained the government departments and treasury. Today it is open to the public and is still home to Thailand's most sacred place of worship, the Temple of the Emerald Buddha.

Presidential palace

The Hofburg Imperial Palace in the Austrian capital of Vienna was the center of government and winter residence for various empires between 1279 and 1918. Currently Austria's presidential office, the former palace includes museums, the treasury, the Burgtheater (national theater), a library, chapel, and riding school.

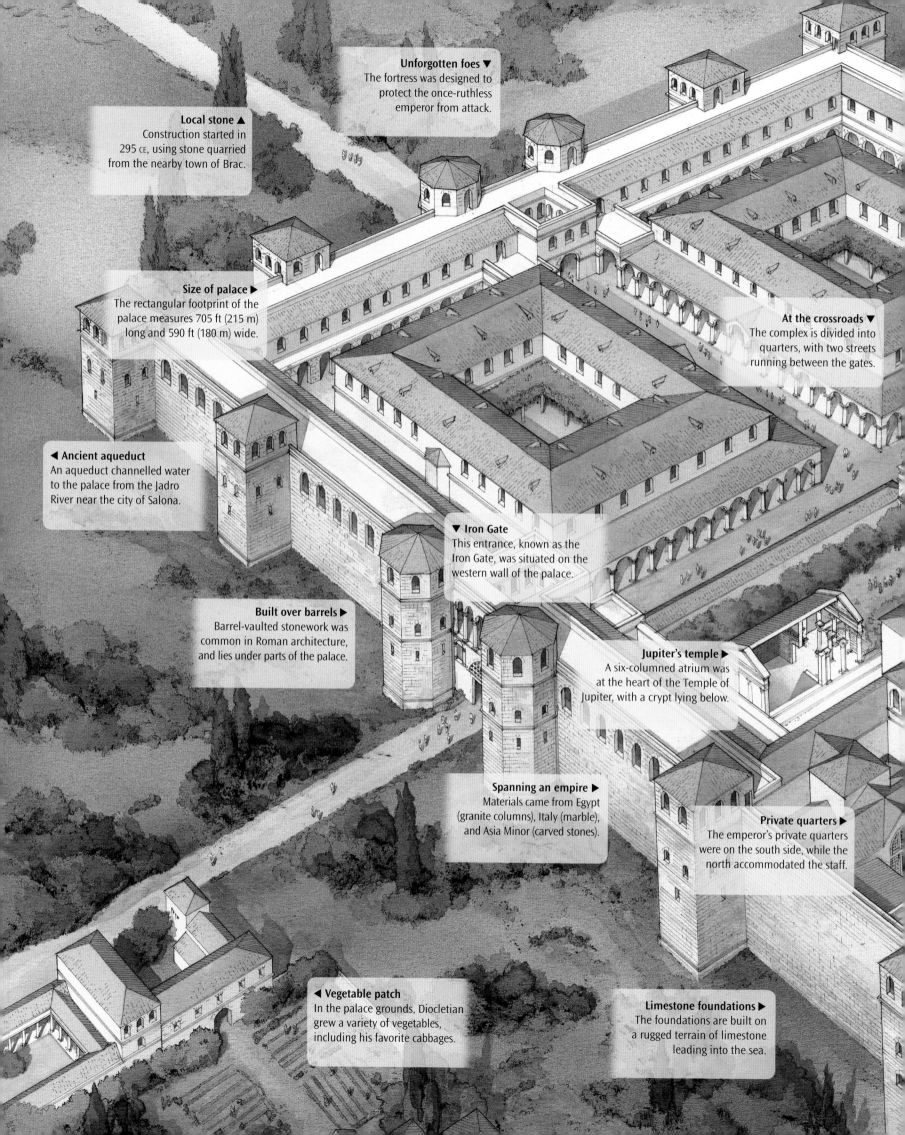

Local stone ▲
Construction started in 295 CE, using stone quarried from the nearby town of Brac.

Unforgotten foes ▼
The fortress was designed to protect the once-ruthless emperor from attack.

Size of palace ▶
The rectangular footprint of the palace measures 705 ft (215 m) long and 590 ft (180 m) wide.

At the crossroads ▼
The complex is divided into quarters, with two streets running between the gates.

◀ Ancient aqueduct
An aqueduct channelled water to the palace from the Jadro River near the city of Salona.

▼ Iron Gate
This entrance, known as the Iron Gate, was situated on the western wall of the palace.

Built over barrels ▶
Barrel-vaulted stonework was common in Roman architecture, and lies under parts of the palace.

Jupiter's temple ▶
A six-columned atrium was at the heart of the Temple of Jupiter, with a crypt lying below.

Spanning an empire ▶
Materials came from Egypt (granite columns), Italy (marble), and Asia Minor (carved stones).

Private quarters ▶
The emperor's private quarters were on the south side, while the north accommodated the staff.

◀ Vegetable patch
In the palace grounds, Diocletian grew a variety of vegetables, including his favorite cabbages.

Limestone foundations ▶
The foundations are built on a rugged terrain of limestone leading into the sea.

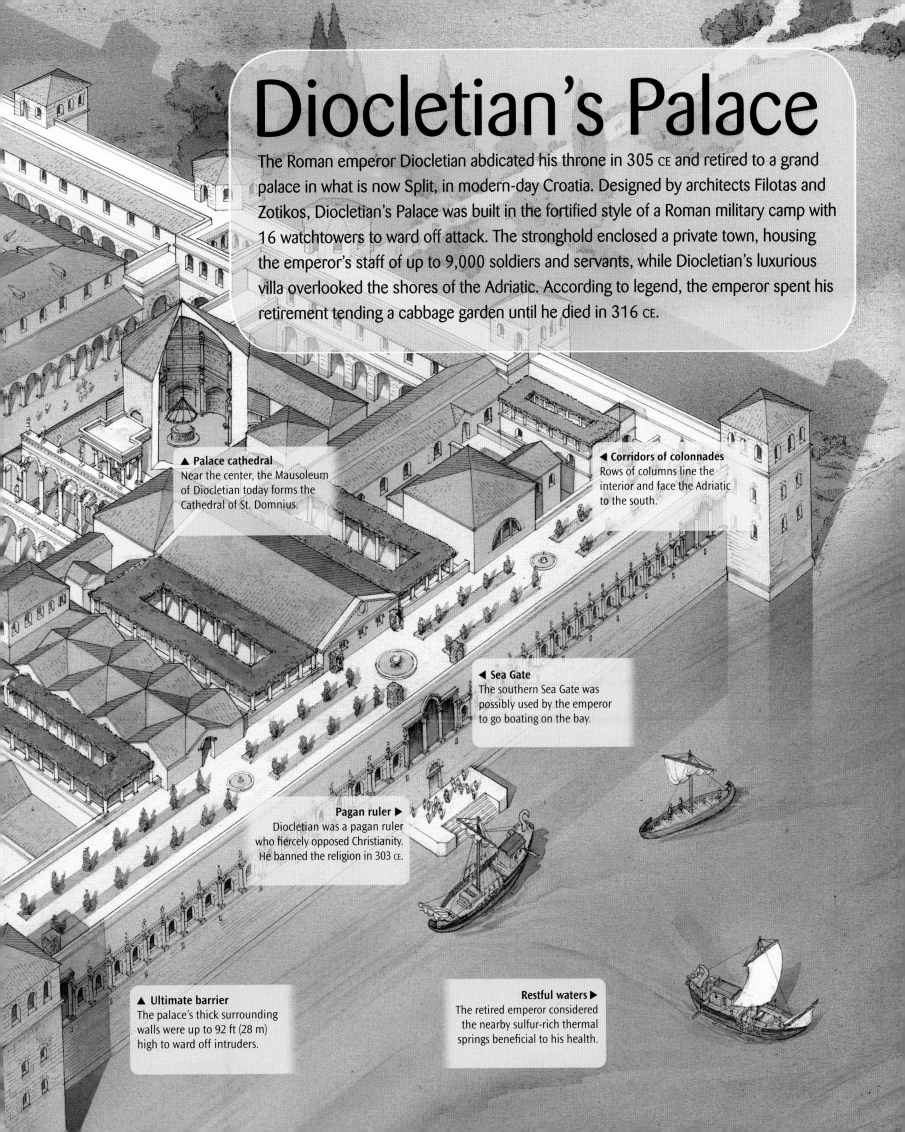

Diocletian's Palace

The Roman emperor Diocletian abdicated his throne in 305 CE and retired to a grand palace in what is now Split, in modern-day Croatia. Designed by architects Filotas and Zotikos, Diocletian's Palace was built in the fortified style of a Roman military camp with 16 watchtowers to ward off attack. The stronghold enclosed a private town, housing the emperor's staff of up to 9,000 soldiers and servants, while Diocletian's luxurious villa overlooked the shores of the Adriatic. According to legend, the emperor spent his retirement tending a cabbage garden until he died in 316 CE.

▲ Palace cathedral
Near the center, the Mausoleum of Diocletian today forms the Cathedral of St. Domnius.

◀ Corridors of colonnades
Rows of columns line the interior and face the Adriatic to the south.

◀ Sea Gate
The southern Sea Gate was possibly used by the emperor to go boating on the bay.

Pagan ruler ▶
Diocletian was a pagan ruler who fiercely opposed Christianity. He banned the religion in 303 CE.

▲ Ultimate barrier
The palace's thick surrounding walls were up to 92 ft (28 m) high to ward off intruders.

Restful waters ▶
The retired emperor considered the nearby sulfur-rich thermal springs beneficial to his health.

Stone carvings

The marble and granite surfaces of the palace were decorated intricately. Teams of craftspeople carved the walls, arches, and columns with typical Roman motifs, such as patterned vines paired with mythical scenes of gods and putti (painted, winged children). The Temple of Jupiter is very ornate, with stunning detail on the main door (left) and picturesque wall murals (above). Some of the most complicated designs were made in workshops on the island of Proconnesus (part of modern-day Turkey), and shipped over to the palace.

Empire State

Rocketing 1,454 ft (443 m) into the Manhattan skyline, the Empire State Building has been a triumphant symbol of New York City since 1931. The Art Deco skyscraper sprawls across an area of 79,290 sq ft (7,240 sq m), with five grand entrances on Fifth Avenue, West 33rd, and West 34th streets. Each year, the lightning rod that tops the antenna of the 102-story building is struck more than 100 times. With a busy lighting schedule covering holidays, special occasions, and events, the exterior of the Empire State Building is here illuminated with blue and green floodlights to commemorate Earth Day and raise environmental awareness. In clear weather, five states are visible from the building's observatory at the top—New York, New Jersey, Pennsylvania, Connecticut, and Massachusetts. About 3.5 million tourists visit this famous American landmark every year.

▼ **Stormy strike**
Although lightning striking the Empire State Building looks dramatic, it causes no damage.

◀ **Record high**
From 1931 until 1972, the Empire State Building was the world's tallest skyscraper.

▼ **Movie star**
The structure has been seen in more than 100 films, including *King Kong*, which starred a gorilla.

Solae tower
Skyscrapers rely on efficient elevator systems. In Japan, the 567-ft- (173-m-) tall Solae tower is purpose-built to test new high-speed elevator systems. The controlled environment ensures that engineers can safely monitor all parts of a lift, including gear systems, cables, and air pressure.

Skyscraper skyline
The densely populated territory of Hong Kong has the world's tallest skyline, with more than 7,680 high-rise structures. Many are residential buildings, home to 50 percent of Hong Kong's seven million people. Each night, 44 skyscrapers in the Victoria Harbour district are illuminated in a sound and light show.

Sky-high romance ▼
Each Valentine's Day, 14 couples can marry on the 80th floor. First, they must win a competition.

Light fantastic ▼
From the 72nd floor to the top, 514 fluorescent and metal halide lights illuminate the exterior.

Precious tenant ▼
The jewelers, Empire Diamond Corporation, has been based on the 76th floor since July 1, 1931.

Elevator to the top ▼
A total of 73 elevators service the building, including six that exclusively transport freight.

▲ Fast movers
The elevators operate a speedy service, traveling up to 1,000 ft (305 m) per minute.

▲ Bird's eye view
The elevator takes visitors to the 86th-floor observatory, located 1,050 ft (320 m) from the ground.

▲ Tragic accident
In 1945, a B-25 bomber plane crashed into offices on the 79th floor, killing 14 people.

▲ Symbolic lighting
Lights represent religious and national holidays, sporting successes, and charity work.

Building blocks

In the heart of Split, Croatia, the historical remains of Diocletian's Palace stand as a reminder of the town's imperial beginnings. Built between 295 and 305 CE, the Roman palace now forms a city within a city, jostling with neighboring architecture. After Diocletian's death in 316 CE, the fortress-villa was converted into government offices. Later abandoned, it was inhabited by refugees during the 6th and 7th centuries. Throughout the Middle Ages, townspeople transformed the building, adding Romanesque churches, Gothic palaces, and Baroque-style lodgings.

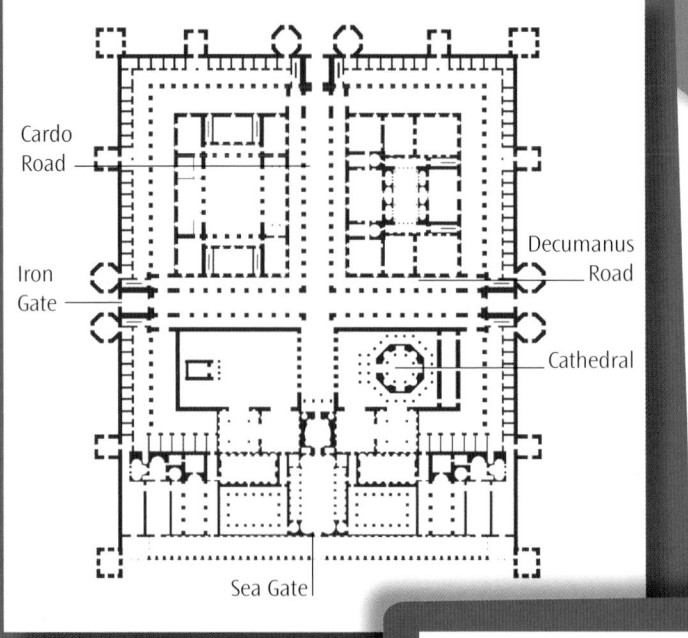

Cardo Road

Iron Gate

Decumanus Road

Cathedral

Sea Gate

Underground chambers
Built on the shores of the Adriatic, the palace foundation rests on karst (uneven limestone). Barrel-vaulted stonework runs like a maze beneath the structure, with strong arches supporting the buildings above. For centuries, the network of underground chambers was filled with rubble. Now cleared, these sprawling chambers have been measured at 75,355 sq ft (7,000 sq m).

Roman routes
Two Roman roads divided the stronghold into quarters, separating the colonnaded structures. The Decumanus Road ran east to west, while the Cardo Road traveled north to south.

WOW!
When Diocletian chose to retire from the throne on May 1, 305 CE, it was an unusual move for the Roman Empire. Most emperors were defeated or died while in office.

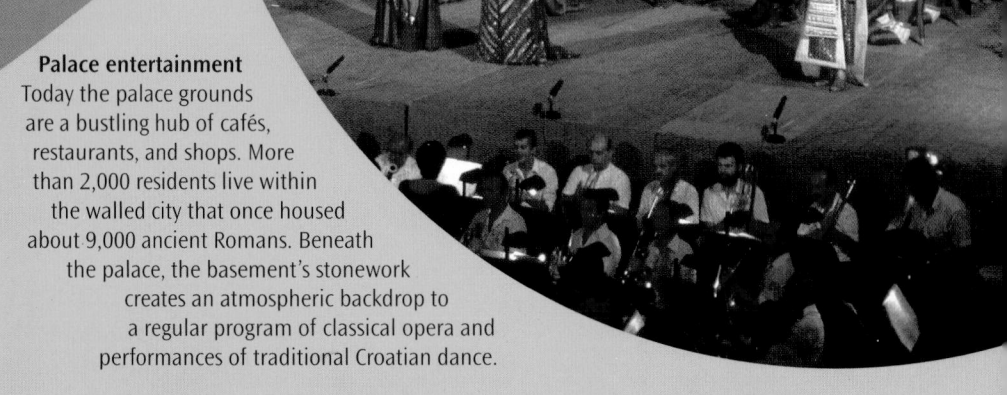

Palace entertainment
Today the palace grounds are a bustling hub of cafés, restaurants, and shops. More than 2,000 residents live within the walled city that once housed about 9,000 ancient Romans. Beneath the palace, the basement's stonework creates an atmospheric backdrop to a regular program of classical opera and performances of traditional Croatian dance.

Skyscrapers

In the 1880s, the world's first skyscrapers were built in booming commercial centers, such as Chicago. Their construction was possible through the development of structural steel, and the invention of the elevator. Today, many modern cities bustle with high-rise structures made of steel, glass, and reinforced concrete. Depending on the size of the city and availability of land, these skyscrapers may be a combination of businesses and residential developments.

Boat building
Built on an artificial island 920 ft (280 m) from the seashore, Burj Al Arab in Dubai is one of the world's most luxurious hotels. The 1,050-ft- (320-m-) tall structure symbolizes a dhow, a traditional type of Arab boat. A fiberglass "sail" shields the suites from the harsh sun.

Stock exchange spectacular
Situated on Reforma Avenue, the most prestigious street in Mexico City, Centro Bursátil is home to Latin America's second-largest stock exchange. The main tower is 267 ft (112 m), with offices spread over 26 floors. The busy trading floor, where stockbrokers buy and sell, is located in the dome at the front of the complex.

World record-breaker
Rising 1,670 ft (508 m) over Taiwan, the Taipei 101 is shaped like a pagoda (a tall, multiroofed tower) and currently holds the title of the world's tallest completed building. In 2004, the supertall structure was the first in the world to pass a third of a mile (0.5 km) in height. Its high-speed elevator system goes to 101 floors, with a top speed of 38 mph (60 kph).

Grand past ▶
The block on which the building stands was once the site of the luxurious Waldorf-Astoria hotel.

Taxi! ▶
More than 12,000 "medallion cabs" or "yellow cabs" service the streets of New York City.

Raised base ▼
The base of the building rises five floors from the street, with the entrance at four floors high.

▼ The long wait
Each day, at least 10,000 visitors queue for up to three hours to enter the building.

Minute movement ▼
If high winds reach 110 mph (177 kph), the building "gives" by just 1.48 in (37.6 mm).

People's favorite ▶
In 2007, the Empire State was voted number one in a list of the US's favorite architecture.

▲ Sparkling windows
It takes four full-time window cleaners three months to clean the building's 6,500 windows.

▲ Total tenants
Once nicknamed the "Empty State Building," 25,000 people now live or work here.

▲ Permanent payroll
About 250 people are employed to look after the building. 150 are maintenance workers.

Building blocks

When President Herbert Hoover officially opened the Empire State Building on May 1, 1931, it was the tallest structure on Earth. Excavation began at the former hotel site on January 22, 1930, with construction underway shortly months later. Steel and concrete foundations supported the 365,000-ton (330,000-metric ton) structure. Completed weeks ahead of schedule and millions under budget, the skyscraper became the star of New York City's skyline.

Lightning rod

102 stories

Planning stages
At the time when the Empire State Building was constructed, a US law existed to prevent skyscrapers from blocking any sunlight in the city. With its staggered shape resembling a pencil or rocket, the formation was designed to lessen the impact of any shadows cast by the towering structure.

Terraced crown consists of seven decorative arches

6,500 windows

Chrysler Building spire reaches 1,046 ft (319 m)

Staggered shape

200 steel and concrete piles

Architectural rivals
In the early 1930s, two of New York City's wealthiest men battled to build the world's tallest skyscraper. Financier of the Empire State Building John J. Raskob was pitted against motor tycoon Walter Chrysler. The Empire State Building won, helped by a 183-ft (56-m) mast.

Grand entrance
The building's limestone entrance is flanked by sculpted bald eagles, traditionally a symbol of the US. Inside, the three-story lobby is lined in marble and granite, with an Art Deco metal carving depicting the Empire State Building as the center of the universe.

EMPIRE STATE

Construction crew
In 1929, the Wall Street stock exchange crashed in New York, causing a global economic slump known as the Great Depression. During this time, the Empire State Building was constructed, attracting more than 3,500 workers. With jobs scarce, teams of men worked around the clock to complete the skyscraper, often risking their lives in the process as they worked, ate, and rested on precarious girders high above the city streets.

WOW!
The towering metal framework was pieced together in just 23 weeks, and consists of 60,000 tons (54,430 metric tons) of steel. Ten million bricks were used to line the skyscraper's exterior.

Dams

Hoover Dam
Dams are built to hold back a flow of water, and Hoover Dam in the US is one of the largest, halting a huge reservoir. When it was completed in 1935, the 726-ft (221-m) dam was the world's largest concrete structure.

Tehri Dam
A power-generating project is underway at Tehri Dam in India, at the point where the Bhagirathi and Bhilangana rivers join. The tallest dam is 855 ft (260 m) high, with its main water reservoir covering 16 sq miles (42 sq km).

Australia's coathanger
Nicknamed "the coathanger", the Sydney Harbour Bridge opened in 1932 after four years of construction. Connecting Sydney's Central Business District to the northern suburbs, the bridge stretches 3,770 ft (1,148 m) across the harbour. Tourists can climb the southern half of the bridge to the 440-ft (134-m) summit.

Bridges

By spanning gaps, bridges enable vehicles, trains, pipes, and people to pass over natural and man-made obstacles with ease. Whether the bridge is a complex system of cables or a simple arch, it must be engineered carefully to support both itself and the load of crossing traffic. They must also be designed to withstand the pressures of strong winds, freezing conditions, and even earthquakes.

Boat-raiser

Scotland's Falkirk Wheel is the world's only rotating boat lift. It enables boats to move between the Forth and Clyde Canal and the Union Canal, which have a water-height difference of 78 ft (24 m). Two ax-shaped arms are located 82 ft (25 m) apart, and can cradle up to eight boats. The transfer cycle takes 20 minutes to complete.

Canal crossing

The 68-ft (21-m) wide Corinth Canal in Greece provides a route for small ships to be towed out to sea. A railroad bridge crosses the canal 190 ft (58 m) above the waterline, with a series of fully submersible bridges serving road users.

Bridge revival

Destroyed by war in 1993, Bosnia-Herzegovina's original Old Bridge was built in 1556 and served the town of Mostar for 437 years. The rebuilt bridge opened in 2004, closely resembling the original single-arch structure. At its highest point, the bridge hovers 78 ft (24 m) over the Neretva River.

Millau Viaduct

Bridging the busy A75 motorway in the south of France, the Millau Viaduct skims over the Tarn River like a spider's web spun in the clouds. As the tallest vehicular bridge in the world, the road deck hovers 885 ft (270 m) above the gorge, with the highest mast stretching 1,125 ft (343 m). French engineer Michel Virlogeux worked with British architect Sir Norman Foster to design the cable-stayed structure. It was inaugurated by President Jacques Chirac on December 14, 2006, and opened to traffic two days later.

Heading south ▼
The A75 north–south route is popular with vacationers traveling from Paris to Spain.

◀ Toll plaza
The toll plaza and management offices are located 4 miles (6 km) north of the bridge.

Hooked up ▼
Maintenance and safety crews communicate via 357 telephone sockets along the bridge.

Help at hand ▼
Patrol officers travel along the bridge to help drivers involved in car accidents or breakdowns.

◀ Modified tarmac
About 10 tons (9,000 metric tons) of bitumen was laid on the road, with a thickness of 2 in (6 cm).

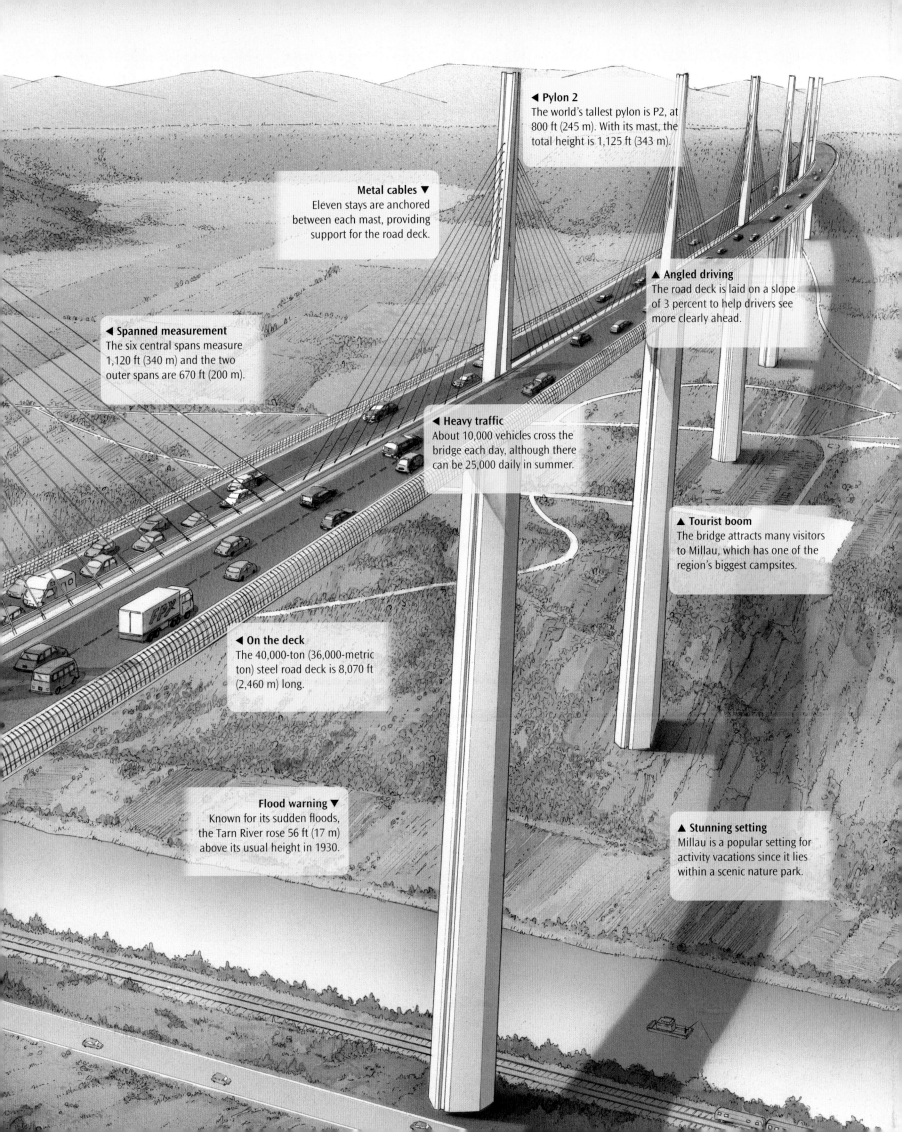

◀ **Pylon 2**
The world's tallest pylon is P2, at 800 ft (245 m). With its mast, the total height is 1,125 ft (343 m).

Metal cables ▼
Eleven stays are anchored between each mast, providing support for the road deck.

▲ **Angled driving**
The road deck is laid on a slope of 3 percent to help drivers see more clearly ahead.

◀ **Spanned measurement**
The six central spans measure 1,120 ft (340 m) and the two outer spans are 670 ft (200 m).

◀ **Heavy traffic**
About 10,000 vehicles cross the bridge each day, although there can be 25,000 daily in summer.

▲ **Tourist boom**
The bridge attracts many visitors to Millau, which has one of the region's biggest campsites.

◀ **On the deck**
The 40,000-ton (36,000-metric ton) steel road deck is 8,070 ft (2,460 m) long.

Flood warning ▼
Known for its sudden floods, the Tarn River rose 56 ft (17 m) above its usual height in 1930.

▲ **Stunning setting**
Millau is a popular setting for activity vacations since it lies within a scenic nature park.

Building blocks

Before the Millau Viaduct was built, the villages surrounding the Tarn Valley in France were famous for their summer traffic jams. For many years, a bridge was planned to ease congestion in the area. However, the soaring plateaus and plunging gorges surrounding Millau provided engineers with a geographical headache, further hampered by heavy winds reaching 95 mph (150 kph). After a decade of research, construction commenced on the Millau Viaduct on October 10, 2001. Under the British–French partnership of Sir Norman Foster and Michel Virlogeux, 500 construction workers completed the monumental structure in just 38 months.

Careful construction
The steel road deck was prebuilt in a factory and transported to the construction site in 2,000 pieces. A synchronized system of hydraulic rams slowly pushed the deck into place, section by section. Working from both sides of the valley, 23 in (60 cm) was added to the deck over a four-minutecycle. The use of Global Positioning System (GPS) satellites ensured the deck was positioned accurately.

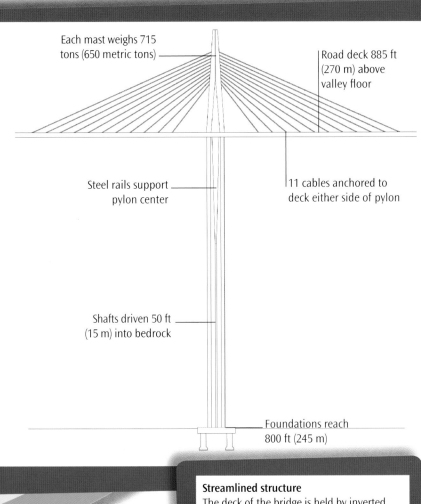

Each mast weighs 715 tons (650 metric tons)

Road deck 885 ft (270 m) above valley floor

Steel rails support pylon center

11 cables anchored to deck either side of pylon

Shafts driven 50 ft (15 m) into bedrock

Foundations reach 800 ft (245 m)

Streamlined structure
The deck of the bridge is held by inverted Y-shaped pylons sunk deep into the riverbed, with concrete supports located on each side of the valley. The structure was designed to use minimal materials, while appearing almost transparent on the skyline.

Cable-stayed bridges

Alamillo Bridge
Crossing a canal in Seville, Spain, the Alamillo Bridge was built for a global fair called Expo '92. The single pylon bridge resembles a giant harp, with 13 pairs of cables spanning 650 ft (200 m).

Rama VIII Bridge
Completed in 2002, the Rama VIII bridge spans the Chao Phraya River in Bangkok, Thailand. Suspension cables stem from a single pylon positioned toward the west bank of the river. The bridge stretches a total of 1.5 miles (2.5 km), carrying four lanes of road traffic and two pedestrian paths.

Panoramic view
Sweeping over the Tarn Valley in a crescent shape, the curved design of the Millau Viaduct removes the dizzying sensation that bridge users would experience if the road traveled in a straight line. The 10-ft-(3-m-) wide emergency lanes on either side of the bridge restrict the valley views below, ensuring that the traffic flow is steady and the road users stay focused, without experiencing vertigo (loss of balance caused by great heights). Side-screens protect vehicles from the region's strong winds, reducing the impact by 50 percent.

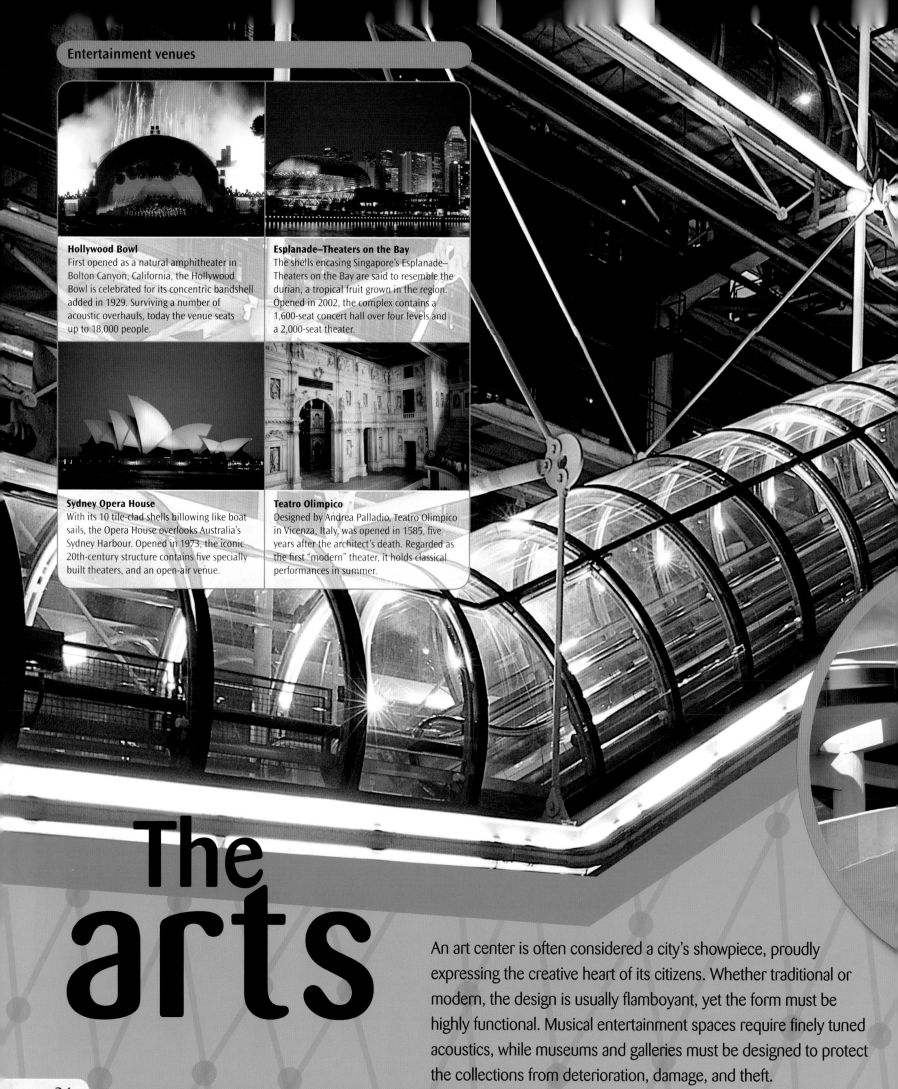

Hollywood Bowl
First opened as a natural amphitheater in Bolton Canyon, California, the Hollywood Bowl is celebrated for its concentric bandshell added in 1929. Surviving a number of acoustic overhauls, today the venue seats up to 18,000 people.

Esplanade–Theaters on the Bay
The shells encasing Singapore's Esplanade– Theaters on the Bay are said to resemble the durian, a tropical fruit grown in the region. Opened in 2002, the complex contains a 1,600-seat concert hall over four levels and a 2,000-seat theater.

Sydney Opera House
With its 10 tile-clad shells billowing like boat sails, the Opera House overlooks Australia's Sydney Harbour. Opened in 1973, the iconic 20th-century structure contains five specially built theaters, and an open-air venue.

Teatro Olimpico
Designed by Andrea Palladio, Teatro Olimpico in Vicenza, Italy, was opened in 1585, five years after the architect's death. Regarded as the first "modern" theater, it holds classical performances in summer.

The arts

An art center is often considered a city's showpiece, proudly expressing the creative heart of its citizens. Whether traditional or modern, the design is usually flamboyant, yet the form must be highly functional. Musical entertainment spaces require finely tuned acoustics, while museums and galleries must be designed to protect the collections from deterioration, damage, and theft.

Pompidou pipes
With its distinctive skeleton of exposed pipes, France's Pompidou Center opened in 1977. It is home to a public library, modern art museum, and music research facility. Designed by architects Renzo Piano from Italy and Richard Rogers from England, the futuristic structure has more than 26,000 visitors each day.

Palace of art
Russia's Winter Palace was built in 1762 as the Czar's winter residence, and now forms part of the State Hermitage Museum. Housing 1,057 rooms, the former palace holds one of the world's largest art collections.

Saucer-shaped museum
Looming over an 8,800 sq ft (817 sq m) reflecting pool, Brazil's saucer-shaped Niterói Contemporary Art Museum was designed by Oscar Niemeyer. The UFO-like cupola spans 165 ft (50 m), and contains three levels.

Viva Las Vegas
The Vegas Strip is world famous for its entertainment precinct, stretching 4 miles (7 km) through Las Vegas. Many of the grand neon-lit hotels and casinos have exotic themes, including the Luxor (Egypt), Caesar's Palace (Rome), and Circus Circus. Undergoing constant development, each building competes to be more extravagant than its neighbor.

Guggenheim

The fluid curves of Spain's Guggenheim Museum provide an inspired stage for its vast collection of 20th-century and contemporary art. The titanium, limestone, and glass structure was designed by the Canadian-born, US based architect Frank Gehry using groundbreaking computer technologies. On October 18, 1997, King Juan Carlos officially opens the Guggenheim Bilbao in a lavish ceremony.

Digital design ▶
The curves were designed by CATIA, a 3-D computer program used in aerospace technology.

Port of call ▶
The museum is located in the center of Bilbao, Spain's busiest port and sixth-largest city.

◀ Shiny shell
Thin titanium tiles stapled to the structure give the museum its shimmering appearance.

Vast museum ▶
The Guggeheim site covers 258,000 sq ft (124,000 sq m) and has 20 galleries over three floors.

Steel snake sculpture ▶
US artist Richard Serra made *The Snake* from hot-rolled steel. The sculpture is 100 ft (30 m) long.

▲ Heavyweight floor
The gallery has no structural columns. Its floor was built to support the heavy artworks.

◀ Sweeping steps
A wide staircase seamlessly ushers people in to the museum's main entrance.

Spider sculpture ▶
A steel and bronze spider, named *Maman*, was created by French artist Louise Bourgeois.

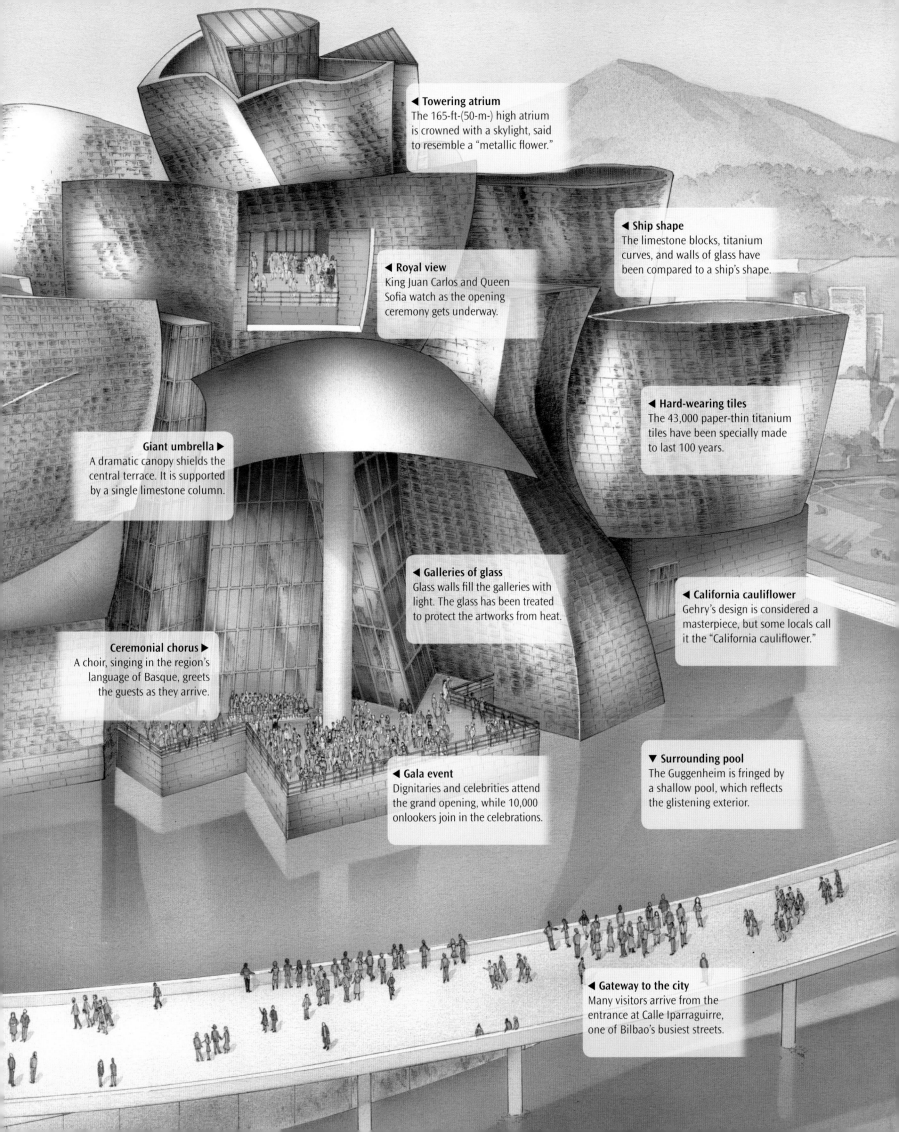

◄ Towering atrium
The 165-ft-(50-m-) high atrium is crowned with a skylight, said to resemble a "metallic flower."

◄ Ship shape
The limestone blocks, titanium curves, and walls of glass have been compared to a ship's shape.

◄ Royal view
King Juan Carlos and Queen Sofia watch as the opening ceremony gets underway.

◄ Hard-wearing tiles
The 43,000 paper-thin titanium tiles have been specially made to last 100 years.

Giant umbrella ▶
A dramatic canopy shields the central terrace. It is supported by a single limestone column.

◄ Galleries of glass
Glass walls fill the galleries with light. The glass has been treated to protect the artworks from heat.

◄ California cauliflower
Gehry's design is considered a masterpiece, but some locals call it the "California cauliflower."

Ceremonial chorus ▶
A choir, singing in the region's language of Basque, greets the guests as they arrive.

◄ Gala event
Dignitaries and celebrities attend the grand opening, while 10,000 onlookers join in the celebrations.

▼ Surrounding pool
The Guggenheim is fringed by a shallow pool, which reflects the glistening exterior.

◄ Gateway to the city
Many visitors arrive from the entrance at Calle Iparraguirre, one of Bilbao's busiest streets.

Building blocks

Described as "archisculpture," Frank Gehry's revolutionary design of the Guggenheim Bilbao is a blend of fine art and architecture. Pierced by Bilbao's busiest motorway, the 349,800-sq-ft (32,500-sq-m) construction site posed a challenge for architects, with its 52-ft (16-m) drop between the waterfront and the city. Across uneven ground, the sprawling museum consists of limestone and titanium blocks bridged by curved sheets of glass. Building on the former dockland site began in October 1993.

Organic shapes
The heart of the Guggenheim Bilbao is the glass atrium (shown above from underneath), with the museum's 20 galleries spanning out of the central space like petals on a flower. Although there are glass lifts, visitors can cross the three floors on curved walkways and stairs (shown right) that wind through the galleries' organic shapes. Giant white beams support the ceilings, reaching up to 85 ft (26 m) in the most cavernous spaces.

Titanium technology
Developed for aerospace technologies, titanium is often used in the construction of aircraft. The Guggenheim Bilbao is the world's largest titanium-clad building, with 66 tons (60 metric tons) of the metal stretching 344,000 sq ft (31,950 sq m).

WOW!
The exterior looks jumbled up, but different types of galleries can be identified. Ten classic rectangular galleries have limestone fronts, while the odd-shaped galleries are covered in titanium.

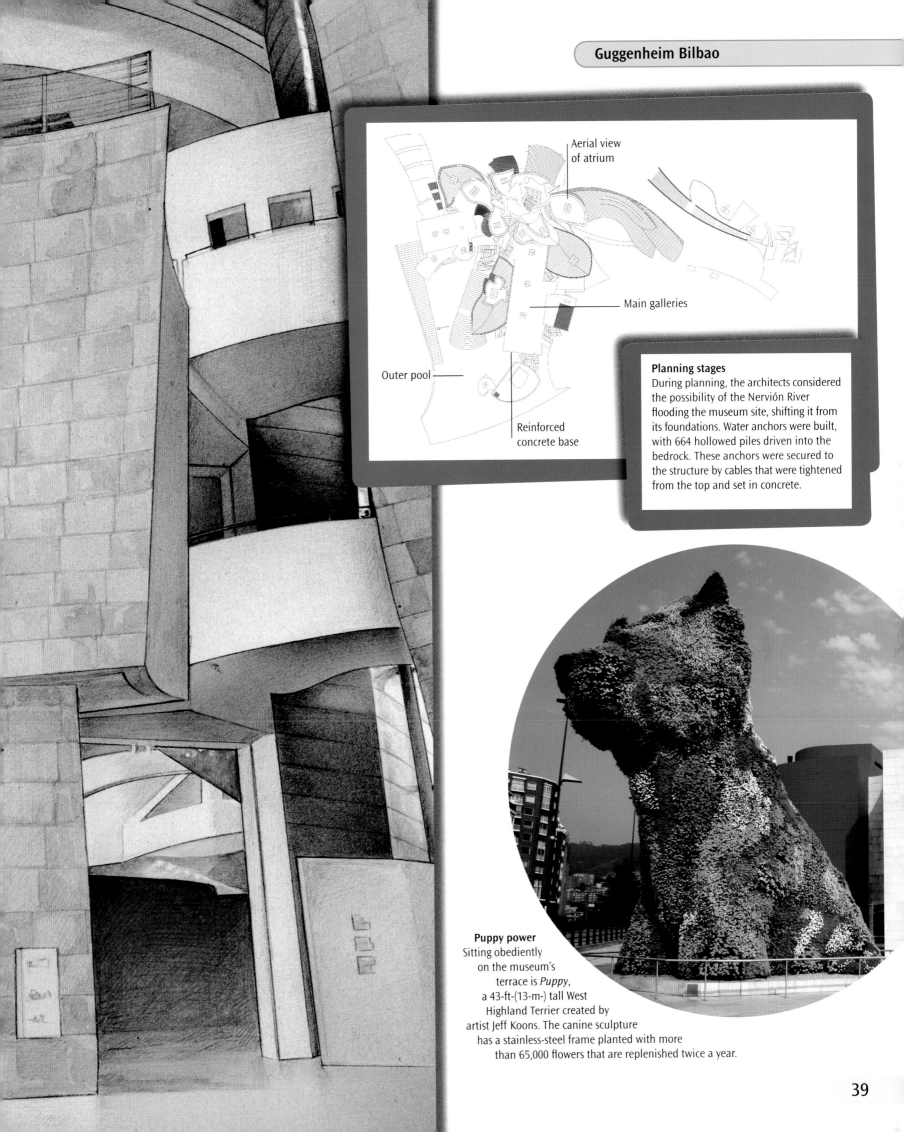

Aerial view
of atrium

Main galleries

Outer pool

Reinforced
concrete base

Planning stages
During planning, the architects considered the possibility of the Nervión River flooding the museum site, shifting it from its foundations. Water anchors were built, with 664 hollowed piles driven into the bedrock. These anchors were secured to the structure by cables that were tightened from the top and set in concrete.

Puppy power
Sitting obediently on the museum's terrace is *Puppy*, a 43-ft-(13-m-) tall West Highland Terrier created by artist Jeff Koons. The canine sculpture has a stainless-steel frame planted with more than 65,000 flowers that are replenished twice a year.

Towers

Throughout history, towers have had many practical and strategic uses. In prisons, castles, and forts, the high viewpoint has helped guards monitor courtyards and surrounding areas. Easily seen from a distance, ports and town centers have traditionally used these tall structures for communications. Beaming lighthouses have provided navigational information to passing ships, while clock towers house giant bells to chime the time for townspeople. Today, many contemporary towers are both tourist attractions and transmission hubs for broadcasting and cell phones.

Paris highlight

Opened in 1899 for an exhibition, the Eiffel Tower on Paris's Champ de Mars is the ultimate symbol of France. From base to flagpole, the painted iron structure stands 1,063 ft (324 m) over the skyline. Three elevators service the first and second floors, with a fourth elevator carrying visitors to the top observation deck at 905 ft (276 m).

Big Ben

Standing 316 ft (96 m) over the Houses of Parliament, Big Ben became London's best-known timepiece on September 7, 1859. As the world's largest four-faced chiming clock, the nickname "Big Ben" refers to the tower's main bell.

Jindrisska Tower

Constructed between 1472 and 1475, Jindrisska Tower in Prague is an example of late Gothic architecture. With three large bells in the belfry, the tower's oldest bell, *Maria*, dates back to 1518 and weighs 1,100 lb (500 kg).

Toronto tower

At 1,815 ft (553 m), the CN Tower in Canada was constructed as a telecommunications hub, providing clear TV and radio reception throughout Toronto. Six elevators travel up the concrete base, taking visitors to the tower's restaurants, topped by the Sky Pod observation deck at 1,465 ft (447 m).

Water carriers

Providing water services to Kuwait City, two of the Kuwait Towers support large bulbous tanks containing 158,900 cubic ft (4,500 cubic m) of water, while the needle-shaped third structure is an electrical facility. At 613 ft (187 m), Tower One contains a restaurant and revolving observation deck.

Spasskaya Tower

Topped by a Soviet star in 1935, Spasskaya Tower overlooks the Red Square at the Kremlin in Moscow. Designed by Italian architect Pietro Antonio Solari and completed in 1491, the structure is known as the "Kremlin clock."

Petronas Towers

Malaysia's Petronas Towers are the tallest twin buildings in the world, soaring 1,480 ft (450 m) high and standing 190 ft (58 m) apart. Together, the identical 88-floor structures loom over the city of Kuala Lumpur. Crossing the towers' 41st and 42nd floors is the world's tallest double-story bridge, the Skyway. The bridge provides an observation deck for tourists, and enables office workers to access both towers. In the Concert Hall located at the podium level, the Malaysian Philharmonic Orchestra is rehearsing for this evening's performance.

▼ **Icing on the cake**
Each steel pinnacle stands 240 ft (73 m) tall and includes a spire and mast ball.

▼ **Transmission devices**
Like most modern buildings, the towers have satellite dishes to receive communications signals.

▼ **Under surveillance**
All 88 floors are monitored by closed-circuit television, and audio alarm systems.

▼ **Recreation time**
KLCC Park lies behind the site, with its exercise circuit, fountain, wading pools, and playground.

▼ **Invisible gates**
Inside the towers, human movement is registered by invisible gates on every floor.

Petronas property ▶
Tower One's office space is occupied by Petronas, Malaysia's national petroleum corporation.

Maxis Tower ▶
Completed in 1998, the Maxis Tower houses a communications company over 49 floors.

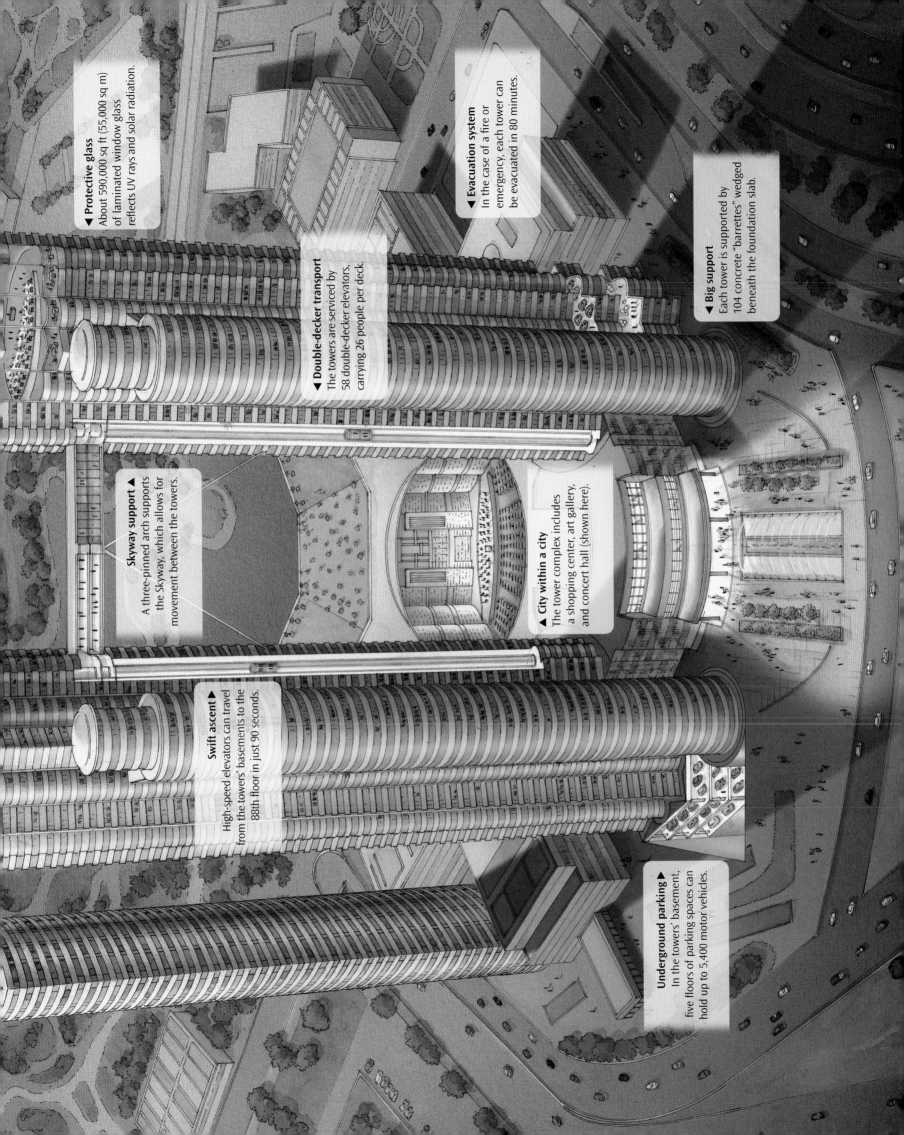

▼ Protective glass
About 590,000 sq ft (55,000 sq m) of laminated window glass reflects UV rays and solar radiation.

▼ Evacuation system
In the case of a fire or emergency, each tower can be evacuated in 80 minutes.

▼ Big support
Each tower is supported by 104 concrete "barrettes" wedged beneath the foundation slab.

▼ Double-decker transport
The towers are serviced by 58 double-decker elevators, carrying 26 people per deck.

Skyway support ▲
A three-pinned arch supports the Skyway, which allows for movement between the towers.

◄ City within a city
The tower complex includes a shopping center, art gallery, and concert hall (shown here).

Swift ascent ▲
High-speed elevators can travel from the towers' basements to the 88th floor in just 90 seconds.

Underground parking ▲
In the towers' basement, five floors of parking spaces can hold up to 5,400 motor vehicles.

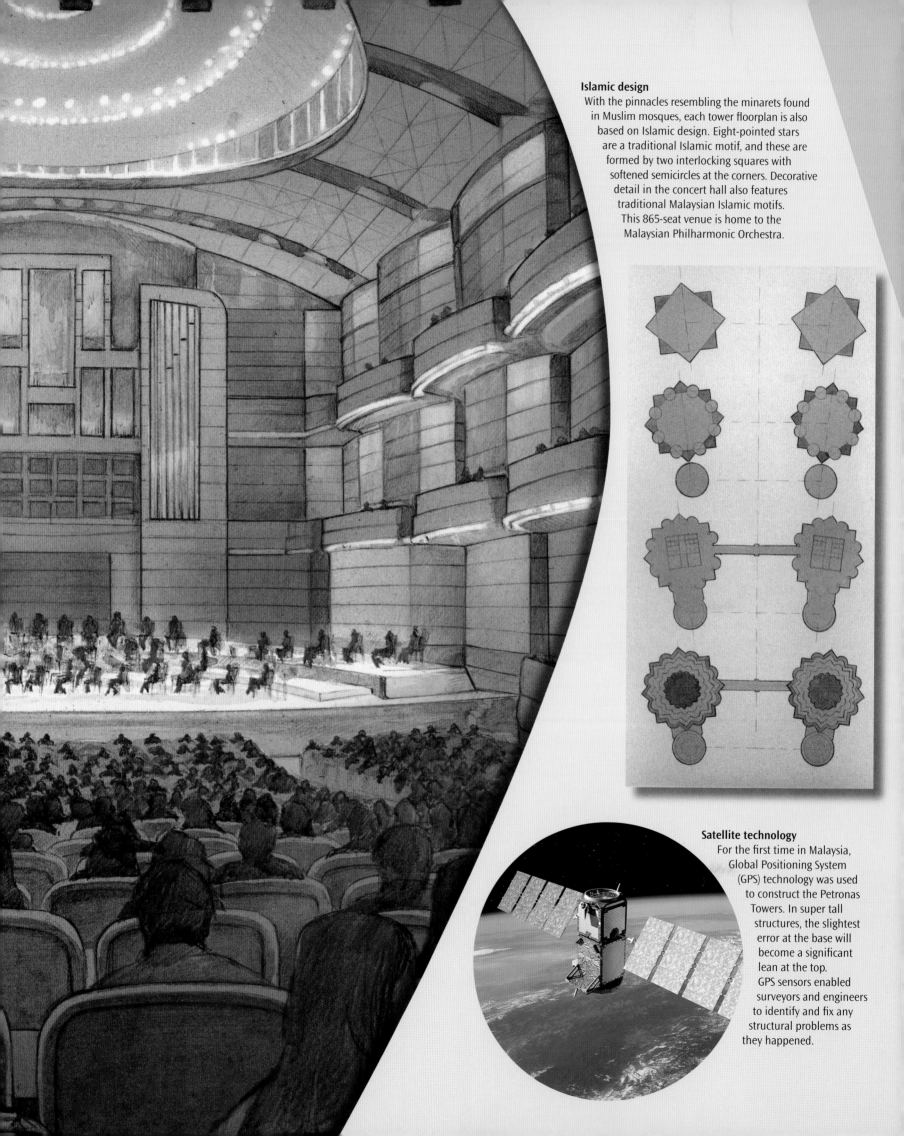

Islamic design

With the pinnacles resembling the minarets found in Muslim mosques, each tower floorplan is also based on Islamic design. Eight-pointed stars are a traditional Islamic motif, and these are formed by two interlocking squares with softened semicircles at the corners. Decorative detail in the concert hall also features traditional Malaysian Islamic motifs. This 865-seat venue is home to the Malaysian Philharmonic Orchestra.

Satellite technology

For the first time in Malaysia, Global Positioning System (GPS) technology was used to construct the Petronas Towers. In super tall structures, the slightest error at the base will become a significant lean at the top. GPS sensors enabled surveyors and engineers to identify and fix any structural problems as they happened.

Building blocks

After seven years of construction, the Petronas Towers were officially opened as the headquarters for Malaysia's National Petroleum Corporation on August 31, 1999, by the prime minister, Dr. Mahathir Mohamad. At the height of excavation, more than 500 truckloads of soil were removed from the building site each night. In April 1994, construction teams began building the twin steel and reinforced concrete structures. With the help of Global Positioning System (GPS) technology, specialized surveyors observed the vertical alignment of each tower at the same time and place every 24 hours to ensure the measurements were accurate.

WOW!
Two rival Korean construction companies were hired to build the towers, and competed to finish first. Structural problems slowed the construction of Tower 1, so Tower 2 won the race.

Tower pinnacle

Each tower has 16,000 windows

Skybridge

Supporting strut

Concrete slab

Soft bedrock

Vertical holes of concrete

Ground control
In March 1993, workers dug deep into the soft bedrock to form the foundations. Vertical holes were drilled and filled with reinforced concrete piles called "barrettes." On top, a 14-ft (4.5-m) concrete slab supported each tower, evenly distributing the weight.

Skybridge
Encased in glass, the steel skybridge allows workers to cross between the two towers, and provides an observation deck for tourists. Suspended 558 ft (170 m) above the ground, the walkway spans 192 ft (58 m). Three struts support the skybridge, with each one extending 167 ft (50 m).

Avenue of the Dead
Built around 200 CE, the Mexican city of Teotihuacán was abandoned by its original occupants. The Aztec people arrived there later and declared the city's mysterious pyramids to be the tombs of their ancestors. The main street, called "Avenue of the Dead," attracts thousands of visitors every year.

Catacombs

French catacombs
Underground cemeteries are known as catacombs. When the graveyards of Paris began to overflow and spread disease, human remains were moved below ground. By 1814, millions of bones were stacked here.

Egypt's catacombs
Dating back to 200 CE, Egypt's catacombs at Kom el Shoqafa are accessed by a spiral staircase. Many burial chambers have been carved into the rock, which experts believe was designed for one family, but later expanded.

Pyramids and tombs

Grand funerary structures are built as monuments and final resting places for the dead, often in the form of impressive pyramid structures or richly decorated tombs. Some are dedicated to entire families; others to just one person, usually a royal, religious, or political leader. The inner tomb may be permanently sealed or have doors, enabling access for visitors and worshipers. Structures such as Egypt's Pyramid of Djoser provide an insight into ancient cultures, while others, such as Pakistan's Mazar-e-Quaid, become symbolic of a modern nation.

Six-step pyramid
Dating back to 2750 BCE, the Egyptian pharaoh Djoser's burial chamber at Saqqara rests beneath a six-step pyramid. At 204 ft (62 m) high, the pyramid is possibly the world's first large-scale stone structure. Inside, there are carvings of Egyptian building materials, such as wood, reeds, and mud-brick.

Mazar-e-Quaid
The resting place of Pakistan's founder and first Governor-General, Muhammad Ali Jinnah, is situated in the center of Karachi. Made of gleaming white marble with copper grills, the Mazar-e-Quaid ("National Mausoleum") was constructed after the leader's death in 1948. It stands on a 177 ft sq (54 m sq) platform, which is illuminated at night by floodlights. The shrine is a tribute to Muhammad Ali Jinnah, recognizing all he did for the nation.

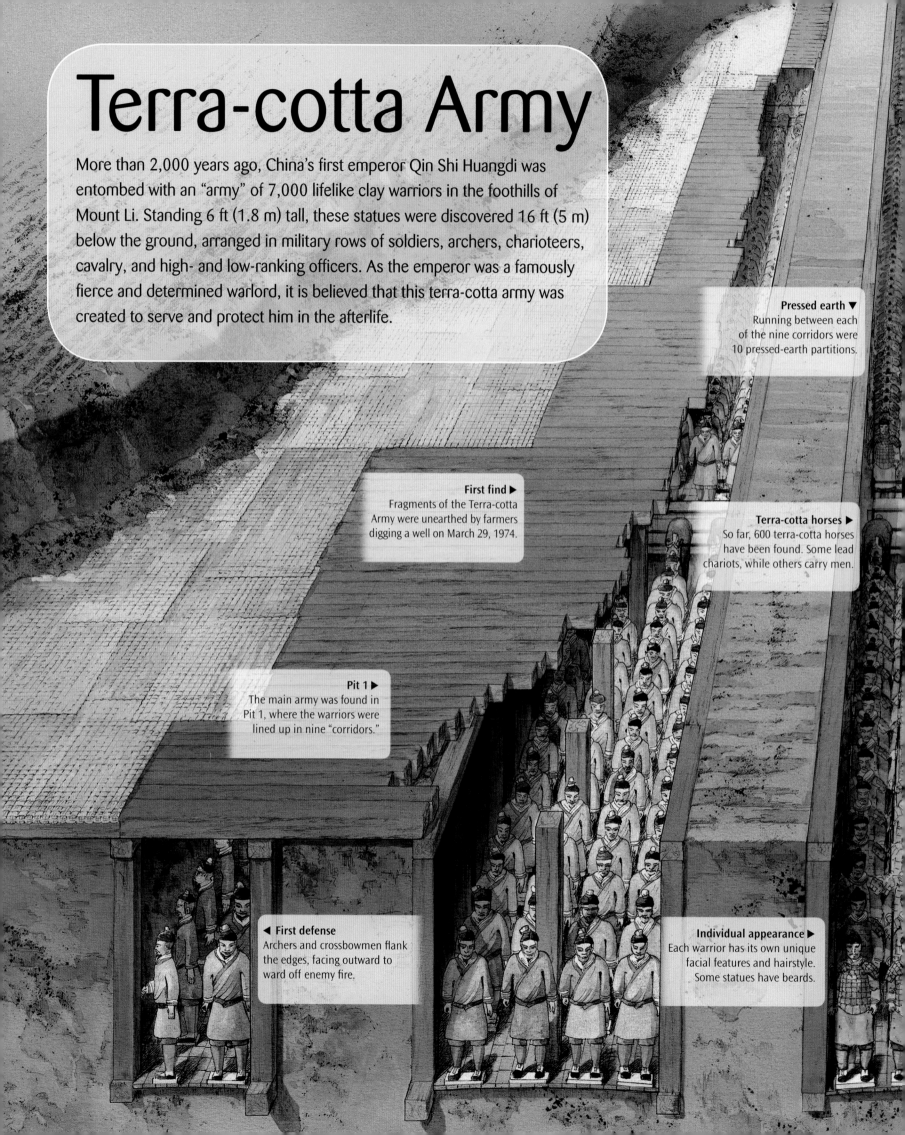

Terra-cotta Army

More than 2,000 years ago, China's first emperor Qin Shi Huangdi was entombed with an "army" of 7,000 lifelike clay warriors in the foothills of Mount Li. Standing 6 ft (1.8 m) tall, these statues were discovered 16 ft (5 m) below the ground, arranged in military rows of soldiers, archers, charioteers, cavalry, and high- and low-ranking officers. As the emperor was a famously fierce and determined warlord, it is believed that this terra-cotta army was created to serve and protect him in the afterlife.

Pressed earth ▼
Running between each of the nine corridors were 10 pressed-earth partitions.

First find ▶
Fragments of the Terra-cotta Army were unearthed by farmers digging a well on March 29, 1974.

Terra-cotta horses ▶
So far, 600 terra-cotta horses have been found. Some lead chariots, while others carry men.

Pit 1 ▶
The main army was found in Pit 1, where the warriors were lined up in nine "corridors."

◀ First defense
Archers and crossbowmen flank the edges, facing outward to ward off enemy fire.

Individual appearance ▶
Each warrior has its own unique facial features and hairstyle. Some statues have beards.

Vast complex ▲
Located east of the city of Xi'an, the complex spreads more than 22 sq miles (35 sq km).

◀ Signed work
More than 80 craftsmen's signatures have been discovered on the fragments unearthed.

Neighboring pits ▶
Nearby Pit 2 held 1,400 infantry, cavalry, and horses, while Pit 3 contained about 70 figures.

▼ Center strength
Heavy infantry in the central corridors provided the main strength in a military battle.

◀ Easterly direction
Most soldiers stood facing east, except those facing outward at the sides and back of the army.

▼ Coloring in
Pigments fade over time, so the colors of the army's clothing in each corridor is partly guesswork.

◀ Measuring up
Pit 1 measures 745 ft (230 m) long (east–west) and 200 ft (62 m) wide (north–south).

Hidden layers ▶
To conceal the army, corridors were covered with wooden planks, mats, and layers of soil.

▼ Battle sounds
Some officers at the front were armed with a bell and drum to issue battle orders.

Armed and dangerous ▶
Many warriors carried sophisticated weapons cast in bronze for use in battle.

Imitating life ▶
Some archeologists believe the warriors represent real members of Emperor Qin's army.

Building blocks

When Qin Shi Huangdi became king of the state of Qin in 247 BCE, work began immediately on building his tomb. About 700,000 laborers and craftsmen worked on the burial complex at Mount Li for more than 37 years, during which time Qin Shi Huangdi became emperor. When he died in 210 BCE, his body was sealed inside the tomb. More than 2,000 years later, in 1976, archeologists discovered three pottery pits containing the emperor's terra-cotta warriors. To date, 2,000 statues have been painstakingly removed from the site to undergo restoration.

Bird sculptures

Emperor Qin's tomb contained many sculptures of birds, including ducks, swans, geese, and this crane, which has painted feathers and a worm in its beak. Crafted from bronze, these life-size figures were positioned in artificial streams and marshes. No two birds were depicted in the same way. Each had its own characteristics and position, which was further evidence of the huge effort that went into creating them.

Restoring the army

Archeologists were first confronted with pits of broken rubble, due to age, ancient looting, and fire. As fragments are unearthed from the pits, the pieces are arranged on tarpaulin mats close to the excavation site. These remnants are taken to a laboratory, where teams of experts clean each piece before carefully rebonding the statues with plaster.

Production line

The different parts of the statues were signed by different craftsmen, which suggested that the soldiers were pieced together, not sculpted as a whole. Craftsmen were probably designated a specific task, such as limbs or armor. Standard molds created the head and body parts, while individually styled faces, hair, costumes, and weapons were later added to the body. Craftsmen worked in teams of about 18 people under the direction of a master sculptor.

Kneaded clay is prepared

Molding a leg

Sculpting a knee

Attaching a tunic

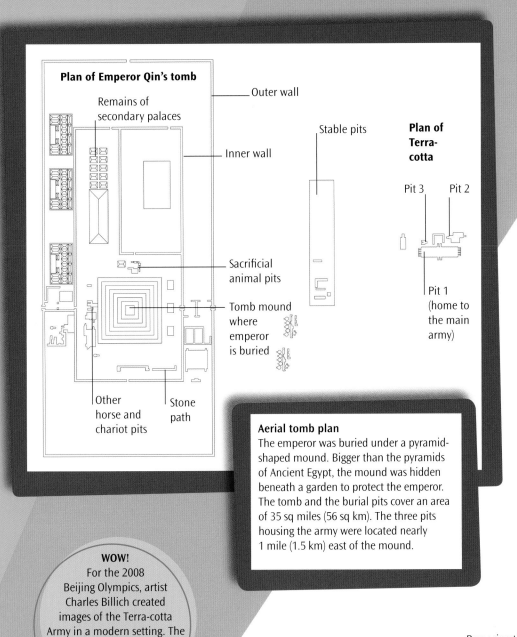

Plan of Emperor Qin's tomb

- Remains of secondary palaces
- Outer wall
- Inner wall
- Stable pits
- **Plan of Terra-cotta**
  - Pit 3
  - Pit 2
  - Pit 1 (home to the main army)
- Sacrificial animal pits
- Tomb mound where emperor is buried
- Other horse and chariot pits
- Stone path

Aerial tomb plan
The emperor was buried under a pyramid-shaped mound. Bigger than the pyramids of Ancient Egypt, the mound was hidden beneath a garden to protect the emperor. The tomb and the burial pits cover an area of 35 sq miles (56 sq km). The three pits housing the army were located nearly 1 mile (1.5 km) east of the mound.

WOW!
For the 2008 Beijing Olympics, artist Charles Billich created images of the Terra-cotta Army in a modern setting. The ancient figures were depicted as athletes, playing a variety of sports.

Painted figures
This replica model shows the vivid coloring that originally covered each statue. Over many centuries, the natural pigments used by the ancient artists came loose before melting into the damp soil that entombed the terra-cotta warriors. Remnants of the pigments in the soil, together with microscopic fragments found on the statues, were used to recreate the colors.

Adding an arm to the body

Finishing the unique detail of the face

Preparing the neck for final assembly

Placing the head

Mayan temple
The Palenque complex in southern Mexico contains the remains of many stone pyramid temples, including the temple-tomb of King Pakal the Great. The Mayan civilization worshiped Pakal as a god, laying him to rest in the Temple of Inscriptions in 683 CE.

Synagogue style
Located in Budapest's old Jewish quarter, the Great Synagogue in Hungary is the second-largest synagogue in the world. The Byzantine-Moorish structure was completed in 1859, with two grand dome-topped towers flanking the main entrance.

Change of faith
Surrounded by dense jungle, Angkor Wat in Cambodia was built between 1113 and 1150 for King Suryavarman II. With five shrines and galleries leading to a central sanctuary, the temple was dedicated to the Hindu god Vishnu, but became a Buddhist shrine in the 1300s.

Places of worship

From the world's largest urban centers to its most remote rural villages, structures can be found devoted to all types of religion. Whether it is a church, mosque, synagogue, or temple, these places of worship are sacred places for people who share religious beliefs. Worshipers may gather for private prayer, education, or discussion, or to attend public services and ceremonies such as weddings, funerals, and religious events.

Golden finish
The Golden Temple in Amritsar, India, was built between 1588 and 1604, but its glistening gold-plated exterior was only added in 1830. Officially known as Harmandir Sahib ("Temple of God"), the Sikh temple is surrounded by the Sarovar, a large holy lake.

Onion domes
Located on the Red Square in Moscow, Russia, St. Basil's Cathedral was completed in 1561. Named after a Russian Orthodox saint, the Byzantine cathedral is famous for the "onion" domes that top its cluster of nine chapels.

Religious rock
Part of the Ellora Caves complex in India, Kailash Temple is carved out of a single rock. Dating back to 800 CE, the Hindu temple features a courtyard, three-story colonnades, pillars, and sculptures of bulls and elephants.

Mud-brick mosque
In 1906, construction began on the Great Mosque of Djenné in Mali, Africa. As the world's largest mud-brick structure, the smooth walls and minarets are studded with palm wood to prevent cracking in the extreme heat.

Hagia Sophia

Constantinople (now Istanbul in Turkey) was the capital of the Byzantine Empire, and at its heart was Hagia Sophia, the main Christian church. Emperor Justinian I ordered the construction of Hagia Sophia ("divine wisdom" in Greek) in 532 CE. At an elaborate dedication ceremony five years later, Justinian enters the church on a victory chariot. Overwhelmed by its splendor, he exclaims, "Solomon, I have surpassed thee!" He is referring to the Bible's King Solomon who built Jerusalem's temple and many spectacular palaces.

Curved supports ▲
Four curved pendentives support the massive dome by evenly distributing its weight.

Under strain ▲
The original walls slowly buckled outward under the enormous weight of the dome.

▼ Saintly circle
As a church, Hagia Sophia's domes were decorated with painted figures of saints.

Dome light ▲
Encircling the base of the dome are 40 windows, which flood the nave (central space) with light.

◄ Christian cross
Both domes feature a medallion with a Christian cross at the center.

All that glitters ▲
In Byzantine times, the walls were richly cloaked with marble panels and glittering mosaics.

Decorative detail ▲
The inner walls are covered with marble panels, bordered by a decorative frieze.

▼ Tympanum walls
The flat walls on either side of the nave are known as the tympanum.

▼ Capital carvings
The white marble capitals that top each column bear imperial monograms carved in the center.

Coloured columns ▲
The ground floor and galleries (balconies) feature 107 purple and green marble columns.

▼ Vast floor
The floorplan is rectangular, measuring 230 ft (70 m) by 245 ft (75 m).

◄ Chancel screen
The altar of Hagia Sophia is surrounded by a decorative chancel screen.

Opulent pulpit ▶
The pulpit is plated in silver and gold, and features ornate ivory carvings and gemstone studs.

▼ Special requirements
Worshipers had to be baptized to enter, while women could only stand in the uppper galleries.

Assembly of priests ▶
As the bishop greeted the emperor, a group of priests lined up to give offerings to the poor.

► Hero's welcome
Large crowds gathered at Hagia Sophia's entrance to welcome Justinian inside.

Restricted entry ▶
People who were not baptized could only access the outer narthex (lobby) of Hagia Sophia.

◄ Emperor's procession
Justinian arrived at Hagia Sophia, waving to onlookers from his horse-drawn victory chariot.

▼ Ceremonial sacrifice
About 10,000 chickens, 6,000 sheep, 1,000 pigs, 1,000 bulls, and 600 deer were sacrificed.

Building blocks

At the time of its construction, Hagia Sophia was the largest domed building ever built. Between 532 and 537 CE, more than 10,000 laborers and craftspeople worked on the structure. To achieve his vision, Byzantine emperor Justinian I is thought to have used all the state treasury's funds. The best materials were carted to the site from quarries across the eastern empire, including porphyry (rock containing crystals) from Egypt, yellow stone from Syria, and green marble from Thessaly in Greece. The structure's domes and vaults were designed by Isidore of Miletus, a physics teacher, and Anthemius of Tralles, a professor of geometry.

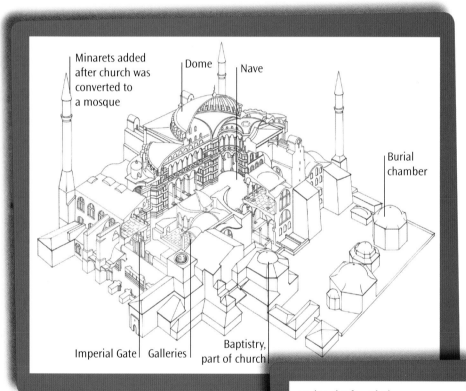

Minarets added after church was converted to a mosque

Dome

Nave

Burial chamber

Imperial Gate

Galleries

Baptistry, part of church

Laying the foundations
Hagia Sophia's foundation is a slope of natural rock. As a result, in 558 and 562 CE, the structure was partly destroyed by earthquakes. Engineers have since found that the brick and lime mortar used in the building's construction and repairs is a very durable form of cement.

Byzantine mosaics
Dating back to the 9th century, Hagia Sophia's oldest surviving Byzantine mosaic is the Virgin and Child. In Byzantine art, religious figures were always shown facing forward against a golden background. Mosaic artists used colored stone, glass, marble, and semiprecious gems to piece together their work, which was pressed into a mortar base.

WOW!
Cannon balls dating back 550 years are scattered around Hagia Sophia as a reminder of the great battle of Constantinople. The Ottomans' powerful cannons fired up to 1 mile (1.6 km).

Transportation hubs

More than 50 years ago, international travel was rare and usually limited to wealthy travelers or families moving abroad. However, with modern advances in transportation, travel has become more accessible as businesses provide luxury and budget services for all. Whether by air, sea, rail, or road, this greater demand on transportation requires sophisticated hubs that can serve huge numbers of business commuters and vacationers.

Island airport
Operating around the clock, Kansai International Airport is located on an artificial island 3 miles (5 km) east off the coast of Honshu, Japan. The wing-shaped terminal is constructed to withstand Japan's many earthquakes and seasonal winds. Planes taking off from the airport visit 29 countries and 14 Japanese cities.

Cruiseship capital
The Port of Miami is one of the busiest in the US. Known as the cruiseship capital of the world, this major port serves 20 international shipping lines, and can accommodate large luxury liners. In 2007, almost four million sea passengers passed through Miami's busy terminal.

Moscow Underground

Every day, about 260,000 commuters sweep through the central hall of Komsomolskaya Station in Moscow, Russia. Opened on January 30, 1952, the grand interior features precious materials usually found in a palace or ballroom. Bronze and crystal chandeliers hang overhead, while white marble columns form elegant colonnades. Resembling an intricately iced cake, the Baroque-style ceiling is painted pale yellow, and trimmed with fine plaster moldings. The ceiling is encrusted with eight gold mosaic panels depicting important military parades and historical figures.

Helpful signs ▶
Signs around Komsomolskaya direct Russian- and English-speakers to information stations.

Striving for greatness ▲
Stalin used the nation's most celebrated architects, artists, and artisans to create his grand vision.

◀ City center
The subway exit leads passengers into Komsomolskaya Square, one of Moscow's busiest areas.

▼ Public palaces
The subway was described by former leader Joseph Stalin as "palaces for the people."

◀ Ticket to ride
A one-way ticket costs 17 roubles (70 cents) with the fare repeated for each piece of luggage.

▲ Greater network
Komsomolskaya is part of a network of 173 stations that make up the Moscow Underground.

Help at hand ▶
Every subway station has a police post and first-aid station for commuters requiring assistance.

▼ Crossed lines
Two train lines run through Komsomolskaya Station, including the famous "Ring Line."

▼ Safety site
Since they were underground, the subway stations were designated bunkers in the event of war.

▼ Molded motifs
The intricate floral motifs dotted over the ceiling were originally cast in plaster molds.

Marble supplies ▼
The subway's marble comes from quarries across the country—as far as central Asia.

Clean sweep ▶
The station is kept free of graffiti and grime with a round-the-clock team of maintenance staff.

▼ Shiny floors
The main hall stretches 180 ft (55 m) in length, and is richly tiled in polished granite.

Structural features
The beautiful ribbed dome that crowns Hagia Sophia is 184 ft (56 m) above the nave and lined with 40 arched windows. The dome was redecorated with an Islamic design (below) when the structure was turned into a mosque in the 15th century. Craftsmen carved the columns with a palm and grape pattern (right).

Hagia Sophia

Religious convert
The Muslim Ottomans conquered Istanbul in 1453, and the Christian church was converted into a mosque. Over time, four minarets were added to the corners of the structure. At the southern corner, the first brick minaret was built under Muslim ruler Mehmed II, who oversaw the church's conversion to Islam. Hagia Sophia is no longer a mosque and is instead used as a museum.

Dome designs

Pantheon
The masonry dome topping the Pantheon in Rome spans 142 ft (43 m). To ease the weight, decorative shapes called coffers were cut from the interior. A column of sunlight enters the building through an oculus (hole) at the top.

Eden Project
The UK's environmentally friendly Eden Project consists of eight domes housing a variety of trees and plants. The lightweight steel frames are covered in a transparent foil called ETFE, so natural light can enter.

Polished to perfection
For almost 60 years, Komsomolskaya Station has been kept gleaming by teams of maintenance staff that attend to every surface as though it were a luxury hotel. The brass and crystal chandeliers are regularly polished, while the marble entrance is treated frequently to keep it free of grime.

Going underground
The Moscow subway's first underground line, Sokolnicheskaya, was dug by thousands of workers recruited from the Soviet army and prisons, as well as volunteers from the Komsomol Youth League. The first stations were shallow, but advances in tunneling techniques meant that later stations could go much deeper.

▲ Arching greatness
The frescoed Baroque ceiling forms a grand arch stretching along the station's main hallway.

Original mosaics ▶
Russian artist Pavel Korin crafted the original mosaics in the lavish style of Byzantine craftsmen.

◀ Lavish lighting
Elaborate bronze and crystal chandeliers hang from the main hall and railroad platforms.

Historic theme ▶
The first stations had themes, with Komsomolskaya celebrating Russia's historic victories.

◀ Divine light
Maintenance staff regularly replace bulbs and clean the brass, ensuring the chandeliers sparkle.

▼ Long way down
At the back of the hall is the subway network's longest escalator, measuring 260 ft (80 m).

Marble colonnade ▶
A colonnade of 68 marble columns skirts the main hall of Komsomolskaya Station.

Car service ▲
Trains traveling on the Ring Line have six cars. Each car measures 65 ft (20 m).

Frequent trains ▼
Stations are free of timetables, with trains stopping every 90 seconds during rush hour.

▶ Right direction
Male announcers indicate a Ring Line train is traveling clockwise, while female means the opposite.

▼ Driver's area
Subway drivers sit in the control room, a small lit compartment at the front of the train.

Super service ▼
Trains operate on the Moscow subway network between 5:30 a.m. and 1 a.m. daily.

◀ Steady flow
Outside of rush hour, the station is still busy with trains arriving every three minutes.

Line 5 ▼
Komsomolskaya is on the Koltsevaya line, which was the fifth line added to the network.

C4

← ✈ ทางออกขึ้นเครื่อง C1,C1a
   Gates
→ ✈ ทางออกขึ้นเครื่อง C2,C2a
   Gates
↙ ✈ ทางออกขึ้นเครื่อง C3,5,7,9
   Gates
↗ ✈ ทางออกขึ้นเครื่อง C4,6,8,10
   Gates

Station style

Taste of the tropics
Atocha Station serves the city of Madrid, with high-speed trains visiting other parts of Spain. Though it has been updated with a modern terminal, the original 1851 station is the main concourse, complete with an indoor tropical garden.

City grandeur
More than half a million rail commuters pass through Grand Central Terminal in New York City every day. Flooded with light from three 60-ft- (18-m-) high windows, the terminal's main concourse stretches 200 ft (60 m).

Bus base
With passengers boarding buses directly from indoor lounges, Nils Ericson Terminal in Gothenburg, Sweden, is styled like a modern airport. Built in the 1990s, the glass and tubular steel station is named after Nils Ericson, a local inventor and engineer.

Futuristic airport
Opened in 2006, Suvarnabhumi Airport is Thailand's main airport. About 18 miles (30 km) east of Bangkok, this high-tech airport is situated on former swamp land. Two parallel runways allow for departures and arrivals at the same time, with the airport serving up to 76 flights an hour.

Building blocks

Carrying at least eight million passengers each day, the Moscow Underground is the world's busiest commuter rail network. Built under Soviet rule by Joseph Stalin, Moscow's first underground line opened in 1935, with 13 stations along 7 miles (11 km) of track. Designed to showcase the best of Soviet architecture and design, the subway has grand mosaics, chandeliers, marble columns, and stunning stucco-covered ceilings. By 2008, Moscow's subway network consisted of 173 stations on 12 lines.

Images of Lenin
In Komsomolskaya Station, two of the eight mosaics depict Communist leader Vladimir Lenin, who was the first leader of the Russian Soviet Republic. This mosaic shows Lenin addressing a crowd in the Red Square, while another mosaic features a Soviet woman holding a hammer and sickle (a Communist symbol) at Lenin's tomb.

Length of 25 miles (41 km)

Komsomolskaya

Subway map
Legend has it that Joseph Stalin inspired Metro engineers to create the Koltsevaya "ring" line (shown brown on map) by placing a leaky coffee cup on the blueprints. When he removed his cup from the paper, the "ring" is said to have magically appeared, connecting all of the other lines!

Length of 12 miles (19 km)

Length of 22 miles (36 km)

Bright lights
Many of Moscow's subway stations are designed on a spectacular scale. Opened in 1944, Elektrozavodskaya has an arched ceiling set with six long columns of circular lamps. Built to celebrate a nearby electric light plant, the entrance is decorated with portraits of electricity's founding fathers.

Big in Japan
The Fuji-Sankei Headquarters in Japan is a high-tech hub of TV broadcasting. Steel-framed towers support a huge 105-ft (32-m) sphere, with an observation deck inside.

Starry sight
Dating back to 1727, Jantar Mantar in Jaipur, India, contains five astronomical observatories. Each stone-and-marble structure is tailored to a different science.

Treasured pearl
Stretching to 1,535 ft (468 m), China's Oriental Pearl TV Tower has observation decks overlooking Shanghai. In the telecommunications tower is an exclusive hotel.

Lavalike lodgings
Antoni Gaudí's World Heritage-listed Casa Milá was built in Barcelona, Spain in 1910. The curvy apartment building has a stone front inspired by the Catalan volcano, Montserrat.

Museum of light
Opened in 2003, the Kunsthaus Graz is a museum in Austria. Its organic shape follows an architectural principle dubbed "Blobitecture." North-facing nozzles line the surface to allow light to flood the interior, while lamps studding the structure create a luminous effect.

Bizarre
buildings

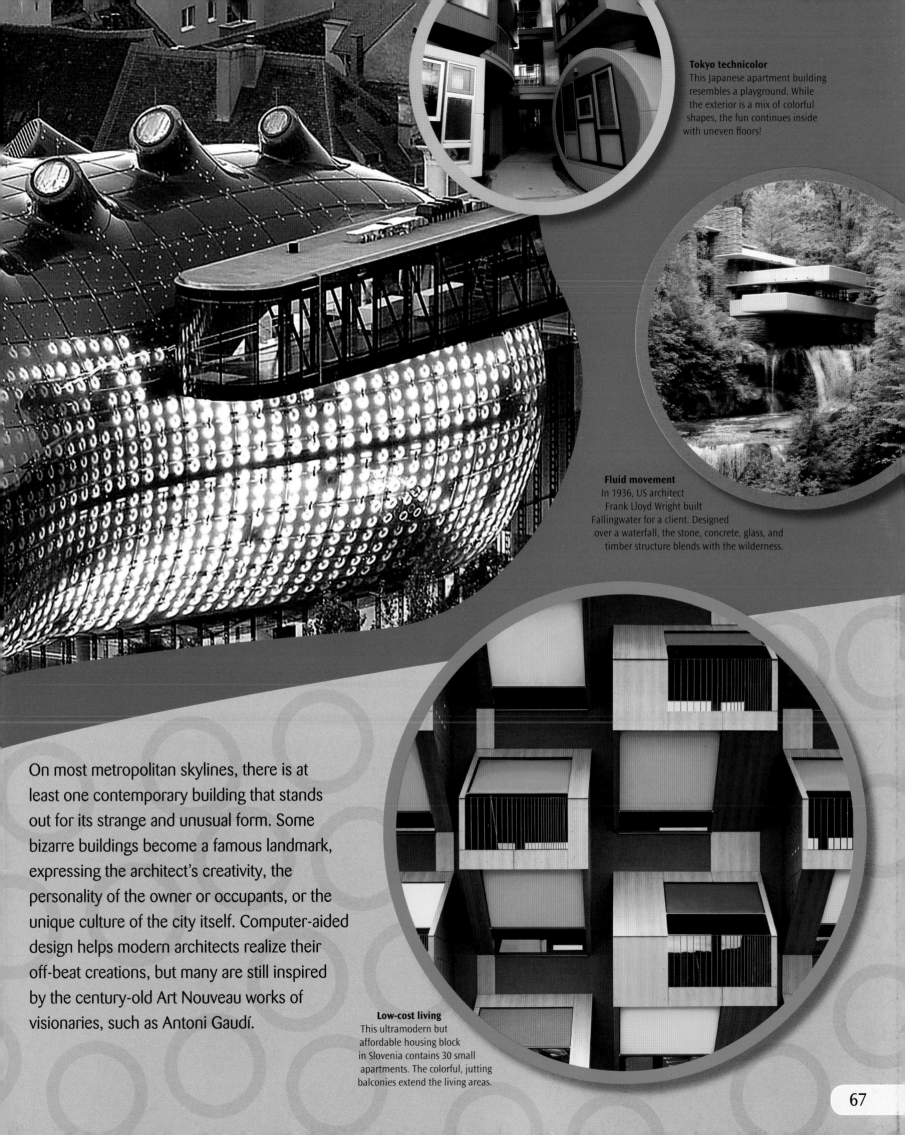

Tokyo technicolor
This Japanese apartment building resembles a playground. While the exterior is a mix of colorful shapes, the fun continues inside with uneven floors!

Fluid movement
In 1936, US architect Frank Lloyd Wright built Fallingwater for a client. Designed over a waterfall, the stone, concrete, glass, and timber structure blends with the wilderness.

On most metropolitan skylines, there is at least one contemporary building that stands out for its strange and unusual form. Some bizarre buildings become a famous landmark, expressing the architect's creativity, the personality of the owner or occupants, or the unique culture of the city itself. Computer-aided design helps modern architects realize their off-beat creations, but many are still inspired by the century-old Art Nouveau works of visionaries, such as Antoni Gaudí.

Low-cost living
This ultramodern but affordable housing block in Slovenia contains 30 small apartments. The colorful, jutting balconies extend the living areas.

Leaning tower

Famed for its dramatic lean, Italy's Tower of Pisa is an engineering marvel and a catastrophe! In 1174, construction was started on the campanile (bell tower) by Pisa's grand cathedral. As it rested on poor soil, the tower began tilting almost immediately after the foundations were laid. Construction was stopped several times as the city-state warred with neighboring Florence and Genoa, before the tower was finally completed in 1360. The new campanile's bell has just tolled, alerting the people of Pisa to their time of prayer.

▼ **Off-balance**
The tallest side of the tower is 186 ft (56 m) in height, while the lowest is 183 ft (55 m).

▶ **Bells in the belfry**
Seven bells hang in the belfry, each representing a single note in the musical

Opening chimes ▲
The large openings in the belfry allow the sound of the bells to be heard far and wide.

Open galleries ▶
Each of the tower's six open galleries features slender columns joined by grand

▼ **Heavyweight landmark**
The tower is 187 ft (56 m) tall; it is thought to weigh 16,000 tons (14,500 metric tons).

▶ **Roman arches**
The tower's distinctive arches were influenced by classic Roman architecture.

Jaunty angle ▶
Engineers tried to balance the lean by building the upper floors taller on one

Little by little ▶
In 1990, it was revealed that the tower was veering an extra 1 in (5 cm) every 20 years.

▼ **Neighboring cathedral**
The cathedral suffers the same architectural headache as the tower—it also has a slight lean!

◄ Marble front
The exterior of the cathedral consists of white stone and colored marble.

▼ Sacred spot
The tower and the cathedral stand on a sacred area called "The Field of Miracles."

▼ Call to service
As the bells in the tower rang out, locals would travel to the cathedral for religious services.

Foundation payment ▲
In 1172, a local woman named Berta di Bernardo donated money to build the tower.

Prosperous people ▲
Wealthy Pisa merchants and noblemen helped to pay for the cathedral and tower.

Keeping time ▲
Temporary clocks were fixed on the third floor of the tower in 1198, but were later removed.

◄ Spiral staircase
From the base to the belfry, there are 294 steps spiraling up through the tower.

Entrance inscription ▲
A Latin inscription reads: *In the month of August 1174, this bell tower was founded.*

▼ What lies beneath
The sarcophagus (stone coffin) of the sculptor Bonanno Pisano rests beneath the foundations.

▼ Bellringer
The bells were regularly rung by a bellringer on the ground, who used a long bellcord.

▼ Shallow base
The tower's original lime and marble foundations were just 10 ft (3 m) deep.

Building blocks

In the Middle Ages, Christian churches rang bells to declare times of prayer. Campaniles (bell towers) were built tall, so that the sound spread across towns and cities. In 1172, a woman named Berta di Bernardo left money in her will for a campanile to be built in Pisa, by the cathedral. A year later, a team of workers and master craftsmen started work on the limestone and marble bell tower. The tiered style drew inspiration from the structures of the ancient Roman Empire.

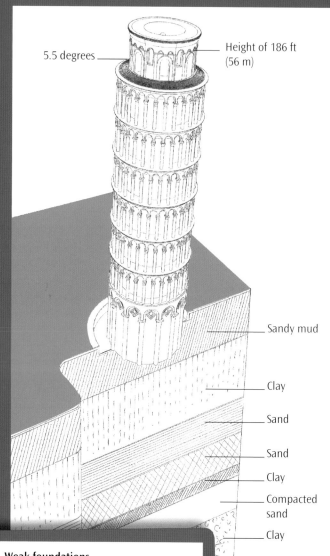

5.5 degrees

Height of 186 ft (56 m)

Sandy mud

Clay

Sand

Sand

Clay

Compacted sand

Clay

Weak foundations
The tower stands on an unstable 5 ft (1.5 m) ditch of sand and clay, which caused the tilt. Initially, it tilted south, but attempts to correct the lean made it rotate! Its most dramatic angle was in the 1990s—5.5 degrees or 15 ft (4.5 m) from vertical.

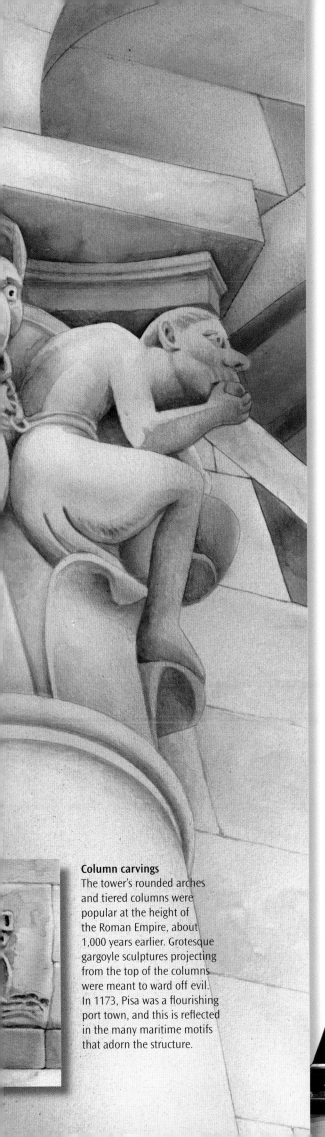

Architectural mystery

The tower's designer remains a great mystery. Some believe it was Bonanno Pisano, a famous Italian bronze artist who lived locally and contributed works to the neighboring cathedral, including the ornately detailed south doors, shown here. Other possibilities include celebrated Italian artists of the time, such as Deotiusalvi, Gerardo, and Guidolotto.

> **WOW!**
> In 1990, the Leaning Tower was closed to the public. It was rumored that the weight of a busload of tourists would be too much for the structure to bear.

Rescue attempts

Lean times
The tower leaned 0.05 in (1.2 mm) each year, until work began in the 1990s. By 2007, the tower was back in its 1838 position. Engineers had dug 77 tons (70 metric tons) of soil from the foundations, moving it by 18 in (45 cm).

Steel support
In 1990, the tower was closed to the public for straightening restorations that lasted 17 years. Here, a crane is lowering metal supports. Steel braces fitted to the colonnade supported the tower's weight.

Shifting style

While Pisa's leaning tower was accidental, some modern buildings are purposefully built at odd angles. Torres KIO in Madrid, Spain, takes the lean to the extreme! Architects designed the towers at a 15-degree slant, dubbing them "The Gateway of Europe."

Monument to Spanish statesman Calvo Sotelo

Each of the Torres KIO towers are 377 ft (115 m) tall

Column carvings

The tower's rounded arches and tiered columns were popular at the height of the Roman Empire, about 1,000 years earlier. Grotesque gargoyle sculptures projecting from the top of the columns were meant to ward off evil. In 1173, Pisa was a flourishing port town, and this is reflected in the many maritime motifs that adorn the structure.

Future
buildings

In times of climate change and an ever-increasing global population, architects are continually striving for new ways to create ultra-modern structures while protecting the natural environment. Many future buildings will be constructed with specially treated glass to take advantage of solar energy from the Sun's rays. Advances in engineering techniques mean that buildings can be taller than they have ever been before, with companies competing to create buildings that rocket high into the sky.

On the waterfront

Floating homes
On Holland's Maas River is a group of amphibious homes. Each wooden structure is built on a solid platform, but with hollow concrete foundations for buoyancy. If the river floods, mooring posts keep the homes afloat without drifting.

Cruise terminal
Located in the Persian Gulf, a Dutch-designed floating cruise terminal can moor three of the world's largest cruise liners. The innovative triangular design has a lifted corner allowing smaller watercraft entry to an inner harbor.

Future entertainment
Sprawling 1 million sq ft (100,000 sq m), the Khan Shatyry Entertainment Center in Astana, Kazakhstan, will be an internal public space containing parks, stores, eateries, and movie theaters in a protected environment. A special cable-net material will flood the interior with light, while sheltering it from Kazakhstan's extreme climate.

Water retreat
Set in a 328-ft-
(100-m-) deep quarry
near Shanghai, China, the
Songjiang Hotel is expected
to open in May 2009. The
400-room resort will overlook
the natural lake at the base of the
quarry, with waterfalls cascading
down the surrounding cliff-face.
Two basement levels will have
underwater views of an aquarium.

Tallest tower
On September 12, 2007, while still under construction,
the Burj Dubai in the United Arab Emirates became
the world's tallest freestanding structure at
1,822 ft (555 m). Although the completion
height is a closely guarded secret, it is
estimated that the structure will reach
about 2,684 ft (818 m). The building
will be a combination of luxury
offices and apartments.

Structure with sparkle
In the Siberian city of Khanty
Mansiysk, Russia, the British architects
Foster + Partners are constructing a public
and residential structure to resemble a
shard of crystal. Jutting from the harsh
wintry landscape like a cut diamond,
the tower is designed to reflect any
natural light throughout the interior,
maximizing the little sunlight available.

First flight ▶
Virgin Galactic is scheduled to launch its first commercial flight from Spaceport America in 2009.

Runway launch ▶
Craft will launch at 2,500 mph (4,023 kph)—more than three times the speed of sound.

◀ Space history
In 1947, Wernher von Braun launched the first rocket to reach space from nearby White Sands.

◀ Organic design
Designed to blend in with the landscape, the shape resembles a slight mound in the desert.

Natural lighting ▶
Sunshine from the bright desert landscape will be filtered into the building through light wells.

Eastern zone ▼
Training centers, mission control, departure lounges, and spacesuit dressing rooms are in the east.

Central zone ▶
In the center are the operations facilities, including spacecraft storage and maintenance.

Sky-high outlook ▶
Huge windows provide clear views onto the runway and spacecraft parking bays.

Ticket to fly ▶
Potential space tourists must pay $198,000 for a single trip on a Virgin Galactic flight.

◀ By popular demand
More than 45,000 people from 120 countries have registered to fly on the first space flights.

▼ SpaceShipTwo
The spacecraft will carry six passengers and two pilots to altitudes above 60 miles (100 km).

Spaced out ▶
The entire spaceport, including the parking and runway, covers 300,000 sq ft (27,880 sq m).

Spaceport

Situated on desert land near Upham, New Mexico, Spaceport America will be the world's first commercial spaceport. The design was revealed to the public on September 4, 2007. Flights launched from the site by pioneering spacelines such as Virgin Galactic will give people the opportunity to travel into space as passenger astronauts. Architects Foster + Partners have made the environmentally friendly structure work with the desert surroundings. The port's design is as a model for future commercial space facilities.

▼ Entry point
Astronauts and visitors enter the structure via a channel cut deep into the ground.

▲ Western zone
Support and administration for the NMSA (New Mexico Spaceport Authority) are in the west zone.

▼ Low-level structure
Set low in the ground, the earth acts as a naturally cooling buffer against the humid climate.

◄ Super site
Spaceport's hangar and terminal structure covers an area of 100,000 sq ft (9,290 sq m).

▼ Viewing gallery
An open gallery overlooking the maintenance hangar provides close-up views of the spacecraft.

▲ Space splurge
The cost of building the terminal and hangar is estimated at more than $30 million.

Building blocks

With its streamlined curves and disklike design, the plan for Spaceport America provides a thrilling glimpse into the future of space travel. Due to open in 2009, the world's first commercial spaceport has very few energy requirements, with the structure using the surrounding desert as a source of environmentally sustainable energy. Set low into the ground, the building will be cooled by underlying rocks, while the rolling concrete roof will use the Sun's rays for naturally generated light and electricity.

Spaceport entrance
An open-cut corridor takes staff and visitors into the building, surrounded by walls documenting the history of space exploration. The path continues past the hangar, before opening into the passenger terminal. Here, 50 ft (15 m) windows provide panoramic views of the 11,810-ft (3,600-m) runway.

Spacecraft
parking area

Skylights in roof

Entrance
corridor

Flying saucer
shape

Sci-fi structure
From above, the low-lying structure reflects the futuristic shape of an Unidentified Flying Object (UFO) seen in science fiction films. The floorplan is arranged with an open flow between the working areas and public spaces. Access to the control rooms is strictly limited.

Heating and cooling
Opened in 2005, the Copenhagen Opera House in Denmark has an environmentally friendly heating and cooling system designed to minimize energy waste. When large audiences gather, the temperature changes dramatically. To stop this, the floor is embedded with 60,000 ft (18,000 m) of coiled climate-controlled pipe. Spaceport will use a similar heating and cooling system in its flooring.

Ideal location
Construction is taking place 45 miles (72 km) north of La Cruces, and 30 miles (48 km) east of Truth or Consequences in the New Mexico desert. The distance from neighboring towns provides room for expansion, while lessening the impact of any noise generated from the facility.

Cheese grater
Nicknamed the "cheese grater," the COR Building in Miami, Florida, uses similar green technologies planned for Spaceport America. Due for completion in 2010, this residential structure will provide thermal insulation, with photovoltaic panels generating solar electricity from the region's plentiful sunlight.

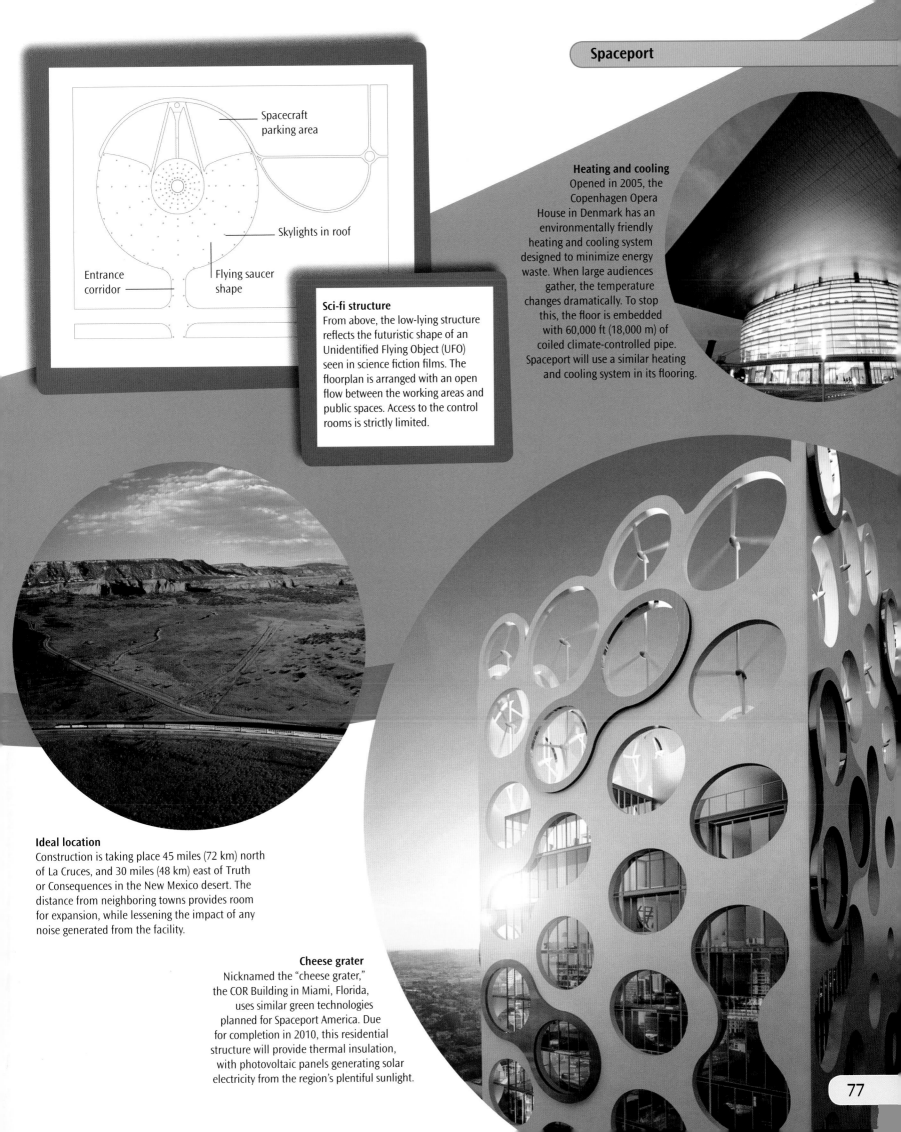

Glossary

altar
Raised sacred structure where religious ceremonies take place. Found in a church, temple, or shrine.

arcade
Decorative row of arches supported by columns. May be freestanding, attached to a wall, or multilevel.

arch
Semicircular, pointed, or square construction that spans an opening, such as a doorway or gate.

archeologist
Scientist who studies past civilizations by searching for and examining artifacts and remains.

architect
Professional who creates the concept for homes and other types of buildings, draws the designs, and oversees the construction process.

Art Deco
Architectural and decorative style popular in the 1920s and 1930s, using geometric shapes, sharp lines, and streamlined curves.

Art Nouveau
Art, architectural, and decorative style popular from the 1890s to 1920s, using flowers, leaves, and flowing lines.

atrium
Large light-filled space in a building that opens to the ceiling. Usually has a glass ceiling.

Baroque
Dramatic architectural and decorative style of the 17th century, using rich materials to display grandeur and flamboyance.

battlement
Short wall on top of a castle or fort with spaces for firing arrows, cannons, or guns. Also called a crenellation.

bedrock
Solid rock layer at the Earth's crust that underlies the soil and loose rocks.

blueprints
Highly detailed technical plans drawn to scale. In architecture, blueprints show foundations, elevations, floor plans, and plumbing, as well as electrical, mechanical, and construction details.

buttress
Structure built to provide added support or strength to a high wall, arch, or vault.

Byzantine
Eastern Roman Empire based in Constantinople (now Istanbul in Turkey) from 330 to 1440 CE.

cable-stayed
Metal cables that extend from several points on a flat surface (such as a bridge) supported by a mast (or series of masts).

cantilever
Structures that project horizontally, supported at one end. A cantilever bridge may use trusses or box girders for added strength.

capital
Decorative top of a column or pillar.

colonnade
A row of columns.

colossus
A larger-than-life statue, usually depicting a god, king, or powerful figure. May hold armor and weapons.

Corinthian column
An Ancient Greek architectural style later used by the Romans. Features an ornate capital (top), carved with acanthus leaves, and a slender, fluted pillar.

dam
A barrier across moving water that redirects, stops, or slows the flow, forming a reservoir or lake.

Doric column
An Ancient Greek architectural style later used by the Romans. Features plain saucer-shaped capital (top) and thick, fluted pillar.

engineer (structural)
Person who uses scientific and mathematical knowledge to design, construct, and maintain the structural components of a building.

exoskeleton
An external skeleton or covering providing outside protection and support.

fiberglass
Material of fine glass fibers set in plastic resin. Strong, light, and nonflammable.

fortress/fortification
Defensive military building or complex of buildings with tall, solid walls, battlements, and weaponry to keep invaders out.

foundations
Lowest form of support for a building.

foyer
A large entrance hall or reception area in a building.

funerary
Relating to a grave or burial. Funerary goods are items that are buried with the dead.

Gothic
A style of architecture originating in France and popular in Europe from the 12th to 16th centuries. Notable for ribbed vaults and pointed arches. Gothic revivals began in mid-18th century England and continued into the 20th century.

hydraulic
Machinery powered by the pressure of oil, water, or another fluid.

Ionic column
An Ancient Greek architectural style later used by the Romans. Features scrolled capital (top) and slender, fluted pillar.

limestone
Porous calcium-filled rock formed over thousands of years from the remains of marine animals.

lobby
An entrance hall or reception area in a building.

medieval
Period of European history relating to the Middle Ages (after the Roman Empire and before the Renaissance).

minaret
Tower attached to a Muslim mosque, used to call prayer times.

moat
Deep, water-filled ditch surrounding a structure (usually a castle or manor house) or town for defensive purposes.

monument
A structure built to honor the memory of a person or event.

Moorish
Style of architecture common in Spain between the 13th and 16th centuries. Relating to the Moors, who were Muslims originally from north Africa.

mosaic
Decorative art where small pieces of colored glass, stone, metal, or semiprecious gems are embedded in plaster or mortar.

motif
A distinctive pattern, design, or shape used repeatedly on a structure.

obelisk
Tall, four-sided stone pillar that tapers and ends in a pyramid-shaped top. First used in Egyptian temples.

pagoda
General term for a tiered East-Asian tower with upward-curving roofs. Often located in or near a temple or monastery.

photovoltaic
Solar cell that converts sunlight into electricity. Photovoltaic panels can be used to line roofs.

pile
A column of concrete, steel, or wood that is driven into the ground to support a structure above.

porphyry
Type of rock containing large-grained (and clearly visible) crystals.

portcullis
Protective wooden or metal gate raised and lowered over a castle entrance.

production line
System in a factory where an item is moved through several processes before it is complete, rather than crafted by one person.

pylon
Vertical structure supporting something above, such as a bridge or power lines. In Ancient Egyptian architecture, pylons were the tall gateways to temples.

pyramid
Three- or four-sided structure where the upper surface meets at a single point. Stone or mudbrick structure housing remains of Ancient Egyptian pharaohs and queens.

quarry
A place where rock is mined.

Renaissance
Time of European history at the end of the Middle Ages spanning the 14th century through to the 17th century. Often referred to as a "cultural rebirth" or the rise of the modern world.

Romanesque
An architectural style influenced by Ancient Roman structures using heavy stone construction.

sarcophagus
An ornately decorated stone container housing a coffin.

scaffolding
A temporary wooden or metal framework used to support people and materials in the construction or repair of buildings.

solar
Relating to or derived from the Sun and its energy.

Soviet
Relating to the former Soviet Union, a country in eastern Europe and northern Asia that included Russia and 14 Soviet socialist republics. The Soviet Union officially ended on December 31, 1991.

spire
A tall tower that tapers to a point at the top; a steeple.

stronghold
A strongly fortified defensive structure, such as a castle.

stucco
A type of plaster or cement that is used as a coating for walls, ceilings, and decoration.

sustainable
Material or energy created from renewable resources with minimal damage to the environment; able to be maintained over a long time.

terrace
A raised area of earth surrounded by retaining walls, used in cultivation (farming crops). A row of houses built in a similar style sharing common walls.

thermal
A small current of warm air produced when the Earth's surface is heated. Relating to temperature or heat.

tomb
A burial place containing the remains of the dead.

turret
A small tower projecting from the wall of a building, usually used in defense. May form a lookout or weapons enclosure.

Index

Credits

Dorling Kindersley would like to thank Lynn Bresler for the index and proofreading, Harriet Mills for picture research, and Simone Boni, Alessandro Rabatti, Francesco Petracchi, Tina D'Amato, Alice Miano, and the team at Studio Inklink.

The publisher would also like to thank the following for their kind permission to reproduce their photographs:

(Key: a–above; b–below/bottom; c–center; l–left; r–right; t–top)

Jacket images: *Front:* Alamy Images: Blaine Harrington III br. Getty Images: DEA / C. Sappa / De Agostini Picture Library bl. Guggenheim Museum Bilbao: c. *Back:* Alamy Images: Walter Bibikow / Danita Delimont tl; Horizon International Images Limited cla. Axiom Photographic Agency: James Morris cl.

Inside images: 4Corners Images: SIME/Giovanni Simeone 21cr; **Alamy Images:** AA World Travel Library 38bl; David Angel 52tc; Arcaid 66tl; Arco Images 34cla; Cn Boon 45cr; Dennie Cox 51tr; Patrick Eden 28cla; Dominic Harris 65br; Nick Higham 67cra; imagebroker 59tr; Norma Joseph 53br; Chris MacKenzie 50c; David Noble 26bc; The Photolibrary Wales 33cr; Robert Preston Photography 66cla; Vera Schimetzek 72cl; Paul Shearman 39br; Toni Vilches 66bl; World Pictures 21clb; atkinsglobal.com: 73tr; **Axiom Photographic Agency:** Ian Cumming 20c; James Morris 47fcr; **Bayerische Verwaltung der staatlichen Schlösser, Gärten und Seen :** "Neuschwanstein Castle" by Christian Jank, Ludwig II Museum, New Palace Herrenchiemsee 12fcr; **Cambridge2000:** 59crb; Jirina Cernikova 40bc; **Corbis:** Arcaid 71br; Yann Arthus-Bertrand 46-47 (background); Benelux/zefa 59cr; Bettmann 27br; Jonathan Blair 18br, 19cr; Laurie Chamberlain/ 7tl; Abbie Enock/Travel Ink 46bl; Muzzi Fabio / Corbis Sygma 71c, 71cr; Michele Falzone/JAI 53tl; Owen Franken 57clb; Thomas Frey/dpa 13cl; José Fuste Raga/zefa 8tl; Harpur Garden Library 57cb; Dallas and John Heaton 12bl; Gavin Hellier/JAI 9cra, 29br; Robert Holmes 13br; Jeremy Horner 66clb; Richard Klune 28-29bl; Louis Laurent Grandadam 15tr; Charles Lenars 56bl; Benedict Luxmoore/Arcaid/ 29c; Kadu Niemeyer/Arcaid 35bl; Patrick Robert/Sygma 41tr; Franck Robichon / epa 67tc; Hans Georg Roth 28cl; Narong Sangnak 58-59 (background image); Joseph Sohm/Visions of America 34ftl; George Steinmetz 52tl; Rudy Sulgan 14br; Haruyoshi Yamaguchi 58clb; Emaar: 73fcrb; ESA: 44bc; Foster + Partners: 73bc; Foster + Partners 72-73 (background image); **Getty Images:** Paul Chesley 15cb; De Agostini Picture Library/W.Buss 9tr; DEA/C. Sappa/De Agostini Picture Library 34-35; Mitchell Funk 35br; Amanda Hall/Robert Harding World Imagery 8-9 (background); Gavin Hellier 52bl; Peter Hendrie 34fcla; Photographer's Choice / Gavin Hellier 6br; Louie Psihoyos/Science Faction 21bc; Phil Schermeister/National Geographic 77cl; Stone/Juan Silva 33cra; Harald Sund 41bl; Travelpix Ltd 40tr; John Warburton-Lee Photography: Amar Grover 9crb; **Lonely Planet Images:** John Elk III 14-15; Richard

l'Anson 53tr; Dianna Mayfield 29tr; Mitsubishi Electric Corporation: 20fcla; Ofis Arhitekti: Tomaz Gregoric 67br; Oppenheim Architecture + Design : 77br; **Photolibrary:** Arnaud Chicurel 46cl; Alan Copson/Jon Arnold Travel 8bc; Chad Ehlers/Nordic Photos 40bl; Christian Guy 33bl; Amanda Hall/Robert Harding Travel 34tl; Imagestate Ltd / Steve Vidler 7br; JTB Photo 14tl; Jtb Photo Communications Inc 6bl; Mattes Mattes 57br; Roy Rainford/Robert Harding Travel 40-41 (background); Marc Robin/Photononstop 6tl; RIA Novosti: 65bl; **Robert Harding Picture Library:** Federico Meneghetti/Cubo Images 6tr; Spacelab Cook-Fournier / Kunsthaus Graz. Photo by Nicolas Lackner, LMJ: 66-67; SuperStock: Wojtek Buss 47bc; Ben Mangor 58br; Nils-Johan Norenlind 77tr; Yoshio Tomii 53bl; Renaud Visage 35tr; Waterstudio.NL: Dutch Docklands 72clb; Wikimedia Commons: 71tc.

All other images © Dorling Kindersley
For further information see:
www.dkimages.com